VIGILANT LEADERSHIP

Vigilant Leadership

Modern Business Leadership in the Age of Disruption

Ron C Betta

Copyright © 2024 Ron C Betta
All rights reserved.
ISBN: 9798325295928

DEDICATION

Dedicated to Raisa Diaz, you are vigilant leader, mother and amazing woman. Thank you for being a source of strength and guidance for so many. You have brought untold amounts of love into the world.

CONTENTS

	Acknowledgments	i
	Welcome	Pg 1
1	Foundations of Vigilant Leadership	Pg 3
2	Threat Identification and Assessment	Pg 27
3	Industry-Specific Foresight Strategies	Pg 51
4	AI in Business Foresight	Pg 67
5	Agile and Scrum in Strategic Planning	Pg 79
6	Mastering Weak Signal Interpretation	Pg 93
7	Building Resilience	Pg 105
8	Crisis Management	Pg 115
	Appendix	Pg 129
	Additional Resources	Pg 139
	Are You Ready?	Pg 147
	Tools for the Vigilant Leader	Pg 149
	Checklist for Vigilant Leaders	Pg 155
	Crisis Management Toolkit	Pg 161
	About the Author	Pg 167

ACKNOWLEDGMENTS

To my loving and supportive wife, Raisa. She has taken amazing care of our sons Greyson and Livio. She is the love of my life and absolutely the best person I know.

WELCOME

Welcome to *Vigilant Leadership*.

This book is designed to equip you to lead decisively in a world where disruption is constant, technology moves faster than policy, and yesterday's playbook is already outdated. In these pages, we will focus on the disciplines that separate reactive managers from vigilant leaders: strategic awareness, adaptability, proactive problem-solving, resilience, ethical decision-making, and continuous learning. You will see these ideas in practice through real-world case studies and practical tools you can apply immediately with your team.

My own commitment to vigilance began early in my career, in an entry-level role at a high-profile company. I quickly realized that simply doing my job well would never be enough. Most of my peers were excellent in narrow lanes; few understood how the larger system worked. After getting ahead in my own responsibilities, I asked my leader for permission to shadow colleagues across the operation. I arrived early, stayed late, studied how different teams functioned, and turned those observations into a report on what we were doing well and where we were exposed.

There was no instant promotion or dramatic moment. What did change was how I was seen. I became the person who understood the broader landscape, connected the dots, and anticipated issues before they reached leadership. Over time, that vigilance led to larger responsibilities and eventually to leading the biggest team in the division. That experience cemented a simple truth for me: leaders earn trust and opportunity when they consistently see further, think ahead, and act before the crisis.

This book is built to help you do the same. Each chapter combines clear explanation, focused examples, and concise bullet points you can turn into checklists, meeting agendas, and action plans tailored to your organization. Treat those bullets as working tools, not theory on a page.

As you read, I invite you to measure yourself honestly, identify specific behaviors to change, and commit to one or two concrete actions at the end of each chapter. Vigilant leadership is not a title; it is a daily practice. If you engage fully with the material and apply it with discipline, you will strengthen your ability to protect your people, stabilize your organization, and seize opportunities others never see.

Let's begin.

CHAPTER 1

FOUNDATIONS OF VIGILANT LEADERSHIP

"Resilience is accepting your new reality, even if it's less good than the one you had before."

Elizabeth Edwards

Welcome to *Vigilant Leadership*. In this chapter, we'll define what vigilant leadership is, why it matters in a volatile world, and how it differs from traditional models that rely on slow reaction and outdated assumptions. By the end of this chapter, you'll be able to recognize the behaviors of vigilant leaders, understand the core pillars that support this style, and begin to see how to apply these principles in your own organization.

1.1 Introduction to Vigilant Leadership

Several years ago, I stepped into the role of Project Manager on a construction project that had already earned a reputation for tension and frustration. Before I ever set foot on the site, a senior leader and a few peers warned me that I wouldn't be warmly received.

They were right.

From the moment I arrived, I could feel the resistance. The General Contractor (GC) was guarded, the crew was skeptical, and the atmosphere was thick with unspoken frustration. To make matters worse, a series of meetings delayed my first visit, and the team had already decided that "management" didn't understand them. The previous leader had left them with a poor impression, and I was walking straight into that shadow.

Instead of trying to prove myself with a loud speech or a stack of spreadsheets, I did something simpler: I walked up to the GC, shook his hand, and told him I was there to help finish the job, not tell him how to do his. I made it clear that I respected his expertise and that my role was to remove obstacles, not create new ones.

The turning point came when I noticed a simple, but costly, bottleneck. Painters and electricians were scheduled to work in the same tight space, tripping over each other and slowing everything down. No one had taken the time to truly see it from the ground level. I asked the trades to pause for a moment, listened to how they worked, and then re-sequenced the tasks so each team had clear room to operate. The fix was straightforward, but it signaled something important: I was paying attention.

That day, I made it a point to walk the site, greet people by name, and pitch in where I could—holding a door, helping clean up, loading tools into a truck. I didn't interrogate anyone about their progress or posture as the hero of the project. I wanted them to see that I was invested in their success, not just the schedule.

Over time, the tone shifted. The GC went from wary to cooperative. The crew began to see me not as another disconnected manager, but as a partner who listened, solved problems early, and stayed visible when things got tough. What changed wasn't just their opinion of me—it was the level of trust, communication, and momentum on the entire project.

That experience captures the heart of vigilant leadership. It isn't about a title or authority. It's about being present, scanning for friction before it becomes failure, and stepping in—not to control people—but to support them, align efforts, and keep the mission moving forward.

In the pages that follow, we'll build on this foundation and explore how vigilant leaders think, decide, and act differently from traditional leaders—and why that difference is becoming non-negotiable in today's environment.

Flab to Flex: A Cautionary Tale

In 1995, Bill launched Flab to Flex Fitness, the first gym in his town. With an energetic atmosphere and a strong sense of community, it quickly became a local institution. Members didn't just work out there; they met friends, built routines, and saw real progress. Flab to Flex was profitable, respected, and firmly positioned as the leader in its market.

Success, however, made Bill comfortable. As the industry evolved, his staff raised concerns about new competitors, updated safety standards, and advances in exercise science. Bill dismissed most of it. He believed his reputation and early market dominance would protect the business. "I know what people really want," he would say, confident that the formula that built Flab to Flex would carry it indefinitely.

While boutique studios, private trainers, and online programs emerged, Bill stayed with the same model. Customers began seeking more personalized coaching, flexible membership options, and specialized classes. Flab to Flex offered none of that. Membership growth stalled, small issues multiplied, and the first cracks in the business appeared. Instead of stepping back to reassess the landscape, Bill responded tactically—one problem at a time—without a clear strategy.

As revenue declined, the gym's resilience was tested and found lacking. In an effort to cut costs, Bill reduced cleaning standards, deferred maintenance, and approved marketing offers that overpromised and underdelivered. Long-time members noticed the change immediately. Trust eroded, and many of the most loyal customers quietly left for competitors who were investing in technology, coaching quality, and member experience.

Flab to Flex eventually closed, not because the market disappeared, but because its leader ignored the signals. Bill's story is not about a lack of intelligence or effort; it is about a lack of vigilance. In a changing environment, confidence without curiosity and adaptation is a liability. His gym became a cautionary example of what happens when leaders cling to past success instead of continually scanning, adjusting, and leading ahead of the curve.

Leadership Defined

Before we can talk about vigilant leadership, we need a clear working definition of leadership itself.

Most dictionaries describe a leader simply as "a person who leads" or "a guiding or directing head." Accurate, but not very helpful. Leadership is more than a role or a title; it is the decision to accept responsibility for direction, outcomes, and the people who depend on you—especially when the path is uncertain.

Think about how some respected voices describe it:

- *"Leadership is the capacity to translate vision into reality."* – Warren Bennis

- *"The greatest leader is not necessarily the one who does the greatest things. He is the one that gets the people to do the greatest things."* – Ronald Reagan
- *"A leader is one who knows the way, goes the way, and shows the way."* – John C. Maxwell
- *"Leadership is the art of getting someone else to do something you want done because he wants to do it."* – Dwight D. Eisenhower

Each quote emphasizes a different angle—vision, influence, example, and execution—but they share a common thread: leadership is about moving people and missions forward, not about occupying a box on an org chart.

For the purposes of this book, we will treat leadership as:

The intentional act of guiding people and resources toward a clear objective, while protecting and strengthening the team along the way.

Before you read further, take a moment and write down your own one- or two-sentence definition of leadership. When you finish this book, come back to that definition and see how your perspective has evolved.

Leadership Roots

From the earliest human tribes, people have looked for someone to guide them—someone who could see danger first, organize the group, and protect what mattered most. In small communities, those leaders emerged naturally from strength, courage, or wisdom. Their legitimacy came from results: keeping people fed, safe, and united.

As societies grew into clans, cities, and nations, leadership became formalized. Kings, pharaohs, and emperors held political, military, and often religious authority. Their power was reinforced by armies, laws, and traditions. Leadership in this world was largely top-down: orders flowed from the throne, and obedience was expected, not negotiated.

Over time, new ideas began to challenge this model. The Enlightenment brought concepts like individual rights, reason, and limited government. The American Revolution, in particular, demonstrated that leadership could be grounded in liberty, representation, and accountability rather than inherited power. Leaders were expected not just to rule, but to serve—and to answer for the way they used authority.

Modern Leadership

Industrialization and urbanization expanded organizations on a scale humanity had never seen. Factories, railroads, and later global corporations required layers of managers to coordinate complex work. Command-and-control leadership worked reasonably well in slower, more predictable environments where information moved upward slowly and decisions moved downward in orderly fashion.

The world that followed the world wars, independence movements, and economic reconstruction was different. Nations and companies had to rebuild, innovate, and compete on a global stage. Citizens and employees expected more transparency, more opportunity, and more of a voice. Charismatic leadership alone was no longer enough; competence, character, and vision all mattered.

Today, technology, globalization, and nonstop media have created a leadership environment that is faster, more complex, and less forgiving than any prior era. Threats can emerge from a competitor's software update, a supply-chain shock on the other side of the world, or a single viral video. In this context, simply reacting is not leadership—it is survival at best.

This is where vigilant leadership becomes essential. The rest of this chapter will define what sets vigilant leaders apart and how they think and act differently from those still relying on traditional, slow, reactive models.

Vigilant Leadership Defined

Technology, globalization, and real-time media have permanently changed the demands of leadership. Markets move faster than annual plans, and small signals can become existential threats in weeks, not years. In this environment, leaders cannot afford to simply respond; they must stay alert, read weak signals early, and move before circumstances force their hand.

For the purposes of this book, **vigilant leadership** is:

The disciplined practice of scanning for emerging threats and opportunities, interpreting them quickly, and taking proactive, ethical action to protect and advance the mission.

Vigilant leaders do four things consistently:

- **Scan:** They watch the environment—customers, competitors, politics, technology, and culture—rather than assuming tomorrow will look like today.
- **Interpret:** They connect dots, ask hard questions, and test assumptions instead of accepting comfortable narratives.
- **Decide:** They make timely, principled decisions under uncertainty, even when information is incomplete.
- **Act:** They execute, adjust, and communicate clearly, keeping their teams focused and confident while conditions shift.

They recognize that disruption is inevitable, but disaster is not. Setbacks will come, yet a vigilant leader ensures the organization is prepared to absorb shocks, adapt, and come back stronger.

Zoom Forward

A clear example of vigilant leadership emerged during the COVID-19 pandemic.

Before 2020, Zoom was a solid but relatively specialized video-conferencing platform. When offices, schools, and families suddenly moved online, the company experienced explosive, overnight growth. With that growth came serious challenges: overloaded systems, security concerns ("Zoombombing"), and a surge of new users with different devices, networks, and expectations.

Many leaders would have treated these problems as temporary inconveniences. Instead, CEO **Eric Yuan** and his team treated them as urgent signals. They:

- Addressed security issues head-on, increasing encryption and tightening default settings.
- Rapidly scaled infrastructure to handle unprecedented volume.
- Expanded customer support and communication, explaining changes and listening closely to user feedback.
- Continuously released improvements and new features to stabilize the experience and stay ahead of new use cases.

Zoom was certainly in the right place at the right time, but timing alone did not guarantee success. The company's willingness to acknowledge weaknesses, move quickly, and stay close to customers turned a potential crisis into a defining opportunity. That is vigilant leadership in action.

Where It Hertz

Now consider Hertz.

Long before the pandemic, Hertz was carrying significant debt and competing in a crowded, price-sensitive market. Ride-share services, changing travel habits, and new mobility options were quietly reshaping customer expectations. Yet the company's strategy remained heavily dependent on traditional airport rentals and tourism.

When travel collapsed in 2020, Hertz was hit hard. A business already stretched thin had little resilience. Rather than being positioned to pivot quickly, Hertz struggled with:

- Heavy financial obligations that limited strategic options
- An overreliance on legacy revenue streams
- Weak communication with customers, employees, and investors

The result was painful: loss of confidence, restructuring, and a fight for survival that played out in public. Hertz's story is not simply about a global crisis; it is about a leadership culture that did not sufficiently anticipate, prepare, or diversify before the shock arrived.

Lessons

Zoom and Hertz faced the same global event but lived very different outcomes.

Zoom's leadership treated disruption as a call to vigilance: they scanned, listened, adapted, and invested in long-term capabilities even while putting out immediate fires. Hertz entered the crisis with limited flexibility, slow adaptation, and a strategy anchored to assumptions that no longer held.

The lesson is clear: **vigilance is not optional**. Leaders who build margin, monitor the horizon, and act early give their organizations a fighting chance when conditions change. Those who rely on past success and static plans discover too late that the world has moved on.

Traditional vs. Vigilant Leadership

Traditional leadership models were built for relatively stable environments. Plans were made annually, information moved slowly, and competitive threats tended to emerge over years, not weeks. In that world, it was often enough to be efficient, consistent, and reactive.

That world is gone.

Today, the speed of change demands a different posture. Vigilant leaders do not wait for clarity before they move. They assume that conditions will shift, that new information will surface, and that their first answer will probably need refinement. They build organizations that can sense, decide, and act faster than the disruption around them.

A simple comparison highlights the difference:

- **Focus**
    - *Traditional:* Hitting this quarter's targets and maintaining the status quo.
    - *Vigilant:* Achieving today's results while positioning the organization for the next five to ten years.
- **View of Risk**
    - *Traditional:* Avoid risk whenever possible; move only when forced.

- o *Vigilant:* Manage risk deliberately; accept calculated risk to stay ahead of change.
- **Time Horizon**
  - o *Traditional:* Annual plans, slow reviews, occasional strategy retreats.
  - o *Vigilant:* Continuous scanning, frequent recalibration, and regular scenario reviews.
- **Information Flow**
  - o *Traditional:* Information travels up; decisions travel down.
  - o *Vigilant:* Information circulates quickly across levels; leaders actively seek front-line insight.
- **Decision-Making**
  - o *Traditional:* Wait for complete data, then decide; perfection over speed.
  - o *Vigilant:* Decide with the best available data, adjust quickly, and learn in motion.
- **Response to Warning Signs**
  - o *Traditional:* Explain them away or file them for later discussion.
  - o *Vigilant:* Treat them as early indicators, investigate, and act before they escalate.
- **View of People**
  - o *Traditional:* Employees execute tasks defined by leadership.
  - o *Vigilant:* Employees are sensors, problem-solvers, and partners in protecting the mission.
- **Definition of Success**
  - o *Traditional:* Short-term profitability and operational stability.
  - o *Vigilant:* Sustainable performance, resilience under pressure, and the ability to capitalize on disruption.

This contrast is not about demonizing traditional leaders. Many of them care deeply about their people and their organizations. The issue is that a reactive, slow-moving style that once worked reasonably well now leaves organizations exposed. By the time a traditional leader feels comfortable making a move, a vigilant competitor has already reshaped the market.

Quick Self-Check

As you read on, keep these questions in mind:

- Do I spend more time reacting to problems or anticipating them?
- How often do I deliberately scan for political, economic, technological, or cultural shifts that could impact my team?
- When front-line employees raise concerns, do I treat them as noise—or as early warning signals?
- In my last major decision, did I wait for perfect certainty, or did I move with discipline and adjust as new information emerged?

If your honest answers lean toward the traditional side, this book will challenge you. That is intentional. Vigilant leadership is not about abandoning discipline; it is about applying discipline sooner, more broadly, and with a sharper eye on the horizon.

The Five Pillars of Vigilant Leadership

To move from traditional to vigilant leadership, you need more than awareness—you need a framework. In this book, we'll use five core pillars that support vigilant leadership in any organization, industry, or sector:

1. Adaptability

2. Proactive Problem-Solving
3. Resilience
4. Ethical Decision-Making
5. Continuous Learning

These pillars are not theories for a workshop; they are practical disciplines that shape how you think, decide, and act under pressure.

---

1. Adaptability

Adaptability is the capacity to adjust quickly when realities change.

Vigilant leaders do not cling to old plans out of pride. They are willing to update strategies, reorganize resources, and revise assumptions when new information appears. They recognize that stubborn attachment to yesterday's plan can be more dangerous than admitting, "The situation has changed; we need to pivot."

A practical question: *When circumstances shift, do I defend the original plan—or lead the adjustment?*

---

2. Proactive Problem-Solving

Proactive problem-solving is the discipline of addressing issues before they become crises.

Traditional leaders often wait until the fire is visible. Vigilant leaders look for smoke. They study early warning signs, listen to front-line concerns, pressure-test systems, and fix weak points in advance. They build time into their schedules to think ahead instead of spending every day reacting.

A practical question: *What problem could I prevent this week if I truly looked one step ahead?*

---

3. Resilience

Resilience is the ability to absorb shocks and come back stronger.

Vigilant leaders assume that setbacks, failures, and disruptions are inevitable. Instead of denying this reality, they prepare for it. They build financial margin, cross-train their people, protect critical relationships, and maintain backup plans. When disruption hits, they are bruised, not broken.

A practical question: *If my organization took a major hit tomorrow, how quickly—and how well—could we recover?*

---

4. Ethical Decision-Making

Ethical decision-making is the commitment to do what is right, not just what is easy or profitable in the short term.

Vigilant leaders understand that trust is a strategic asset. They protect it carefully. They refuse to cut corners that compromise safety, honesty, or the well-being of their people and customers. In times of uncertainty, they default to integrity—even when no one is watching and even when there is pressure to look the other way.

A practical question: *Where might I be tempted to trade long-term trust for short-term gain—and what will it cost me if I do?*

5. Continuous Learning

Continuous learning is the habit of staying curious and informed.

Vigilant leaders study their industry, their competitors, emerging technologies, and broader trends. They seek feedback, read widely, ask questions, and encourage their teams to do the same. They know that what worked last year may not work next year—and they refuse to lead on outdated knowledge.

A practical question: *What am I actively learning right now that will make me a stronger leader six to twelve months from today?*

As you move through the rest of this book, you will see these five pillars repeated and reinforced. Later, we will connect them to specific operational qualities—such as communication, collaboration, and data-driven decision-making—that bring vigilant leadership to life in day-to-day operations.

Operational Qualities that Support the Pillars

The Five Pillars describe *how* vigilant leaders think and decide. To make those pillars real in day-to-day operations, you need a set of supporting qualities that shape how your organization actually behaves.

Eight qualities, in particular, bring vigilant leadership to life:

- **Strong Relationships**
  Vigilant leaders invest in trust—up, down, and across the organization. Healthy relationships ensure that people surface concerns early, share information freely, and stay aligned

when pressure mounts. Without trust, warnings are muted and small issues stay hidden until they become crises.

- **Effective Communication**
Clear, timely communication is the delivery system for vigilance. Leaders who communicate expectations, risks, and decisions plainly reduce confusion, keep teams focused, and prevent rumors from filling the gaps. In a fast-moving environment, silence is rarely neutral; it is usually harmful.

- **Investment in Talent and Resources**
Vigilant leadership requires capable people and the right tools. That means hiring wisely, developing your team, and ensuring they have the systems, data, and authority needed to act. Under-resourced teams become reactive teams, no matter how committed they are.

- **Learning and Adaptation**
Continuous learning at the personal level must be matched by learning at the organizational level. Vigilant leaders build habits of after-action reviews, honest debriefs, and process improvement. Mistakes become lessons, not just losses.

- **Culture of Innovation**
A vigilant organization encourages smart experimentation. People are allowed to propose new ideas, test alternatives, and challenge "the way we've always done it" without fear of ridicule or retaliation. Innovation is not an occasional event; it is a standing expectation.

- **Agile Practices**
Agility is how vigilance shows up on the calendar. Short planning cycles, rapid feedback loops, and incremental delivery allow teams to respond to new information instead of being locked into rigid annual plans. Agile practices give structure to adaptability and proactive problem-solving.

- **Cross-Functional Collaboration**
Threats and opportunities rarely respect departmental boundaries. Vigilant leaders connect teams across functions so that finance, operations, technology, HR, and customer-

facing groups see the same picture and move together. Silos are the enemies of early detection.

- **Data-Driven Decision-Making**
Finally, vigilance depends on reality, not wishful thinking. Leaders who rely on accurate data—financial, operational, customer, and market—avoid being caught off guard by trends they could have measured months earlier. Data does not replace judgment, but it sharpens it.

These qualities are not separate from the Five Pillars—they **enable** them. For example, adaptability and proactive problem-solving are nearly impossible without strong relationships, effective communication, and reliable data. Throughout the book, you will see how these qualities reinforce each pillar and how gaps in any one area can weaken your overall vigilance.

Case Study: Vigilant Leadership in Crisis – President George W. Bush and 9/11

On the morning of September 11, 2001, the United States was attacked in a way that shattered any illusion of invulnerability. Four hijacked planes, thousands of lives lost, and a live global broadcast of terror and devastation changed the nation in a matter of hours. It was a moment of shock, fear, and uncertainty—exactly the kind of environment where leadership either rises or collapses.

From a vigilance standpoint, 9/11 reveals **two sides of leadership**: a failure of pre-crisis detection and a determined effort to build a more vigilant posture afterward.

Before the attacks, intelligence agencies had fragments of information about Al-Qaeda's intentions. Threats were known, but they were scattered across agencies, buried in data, and not translated into decisive, coordinated action. The system was not built for rapid sharing or joint interpretation of emerging threats. In vigilance terms, the "scan" and "interpret" functions were weak and fragmented, even though many dedicated professionals were working hard in their lanes.

Once the attacks occurred, the leadership challenge shifted. The question became: *How do you stabilize a shocked nation, confront an enemy, and rebuild public confidence under unprecedented pressure?*

President George W. Bush's response offers several important leadership lessons.

First, he **communicated clearly and consistently**. In the hours and days after the attacks, he addressed the nation with simple, direct language about what had happened, who was responsible, and what the United States intended to do. The message was firm: this was an act of war, not an accident, and the country would respond. In a moment of chaos, that clarity mattered.

Second, he focused on **unity and resolve**. The now-famous image of the President standing on the rubble at Ground Zero, speaking through a bullhorn to first responders, was more than symbolism. It conveyed presence, empathy, and determination. He did not retreat to a distant, abstract tone; he chose to stand where the damage was visible and acknowledge both the loss and the mission ahead.

Third, his administration moved to **reorganize and strengthen the security apparatus**. The creation of the Department of Homeland Security, changes to intelligence-sharing practices, and new counterterrorism strategies were all aimed at preventing a repeat of the failures that allowed the attacks to succeed. Leaders can debate specific policies, but from a vigilance lens, the key is that the response was not limited to speeches or short-term retaliation. Structural changes followed.

Fourth, the response emphasized **coalitions and long-term engagement**. The United States worked with allies, expanded intelligence cooperation, and redefined parts of its military and foreign policy to address a dispersed, networked enemy rather than a traditional army. This required a shift in mindset—from preparing primarily for conventional state-on-state conflict to confronting asymmetric threats.

The leadership lessons from 9/11, viewed through the framework of vigilant leadership, are clear:

- **Vigilance cannot be an afterthought.** The failure was not in the courage of individuals, but in the system's inability to connect information quickly enough. Vigilant leaders design structures and cultures where critical information moves fast and is acted on.
- **In crisis, communication is a primary duty.** People can handle bad news; they cannot function well in silence and confusion. Leaders must provide clarity, direction, and a sense of purpose when emotions are highest.
- **Symbolic actions matter when they are backed by substance.** Standing at Ground Zero meant more because it was followed by sustained effort, not just a photo opportunity. Presence without follow-through is performance, not leadership.
- **Real vigilance demands structural change.** When a major failure is exposed, leaders must be willing to rethink systems, not just demand more effort from the same broken model. Reorganization, new protocols, and tighter coordination are all tools of vigilant leadership.

The 9/11 attacks exposed how costly it can be when a nation's vigilance is incomplete. They also showed how crucial it is for leaders to respond decisively, communicate with strength and empathy, and commit to long-term improvements rather than short-lived gestures.

As you read this book, keep this pattern in mind: vigilance is not about living in fear of every threat; it is about building systems, cultures, and habits that see danger earlier, act faster, and recover stronger when the unexpected occurs.

Case Study: Leading Through a Global Pandemic – President Donald J. Trump and COVID-19

In early 2020, a new virus began spreading across the globe. Within weeks, COVID-19 disrupted travel, supply chains, healthcare systems, and everyday life. Uncertainty was extreme: data were incomplete, models conflicted, and experts often disagreed. In that environment, every national leader faced the same core challenge: act fast with imperfect information, or delay and risk losing control.

In the United States, President Donald J. Trump's administration confronted a situation with no modern domestic precedent. From a vigilant leadership lens, several elements stand out—both strengths and limitations.

First, there was the question of **speed and decisiveness**. Early in the outbreak, the administration moved to restrict travel from high-risk regions and declared a national emergency, opening the door to federal resources and coordination. The White House established a task force, pulled in health experts, and began daily briefings. These moves signaled recognition that the situation was not a routine health concern but a systemic threat to the nation's security and economy.

Second, the administration focused heavily on **mobilizing capacity**. Federal agencies worked with states and private companies to increase production of ventilators, expand hospital capacity, and secure medical supplies. Naval hospital ships were deployed, field hospitals were erected, and manufacturers shifted production lines to respond to urgent needs. From a vigilance standpoint, this was an attempt to rapidly increase resilience—to absorb a shock that was already underway.

Third, a major strategic decision came in the form of **Operation Warp Speed**, a public-private effort to accelerate vaccine development, testing, and distribution. Historically, vaccines had taken many years to bring to market. Under intense time pressure, the administration prioritized speed, funding, and coordination to compress that timeline dramatically. Whether one agrees with every policy choice or not, Operation Warp Speed represented vigilant thinking: identify a pivotal lever early and direct disproportionate resources toward it.

At the same time, the pandemic exposed **limits in national vigilance**. The United States entered COVID-19 with fragmented public health systems, uneven data reporting, and long-standing vulnerabilities in supply chains and long-term care. Communication from federal, state, and local leaders was often inconsistent, leading to public confusion. In vigilance terms, the country had not fully built the structures needed for fast, unified interpretation and response before the crisis hit.

From a leadership perspective, several lessons emerge:

- **Clarity under pressure is essential.** In a fast-moving crisis, mixed messages amplify anxiety. Leaders must communicate frequently, acknowledge uncertainty, and provide a steady sense of direction—even as facts evolve.
- **Preparation cannot wait for the crisis.** Many of the hardest problems of COVID-19—testing, data, supply chains—were years in the making. Vigilant leaders push for stronger

systems, clearer protocols, and better coordination before disaster strikes.

- **Public trust is a strategic resource.** In a polarized environment, every statement is scrutinized. Leaders must balance optimism with honesty, strength with humility, and decisiveness with a willingness to adapt as new evidence emerges.
- **Partnerships multiply capacity.** Operation Warp Speed and the broader private-sector mobilization showed how quickly progress can be made when government, industry, and science align around a shared mission. Vigilant leaders think in terms of coalitions, not isolation.

COVID-19 will be studied for decades as a complex, politically charged event. This book does not attempt to resolve those debates. Instead, it treats the pandemic as a vivid example of how high the stakes are for vigilance—and how costly gaps in preparation, communication, or coordination can be.

For you as a leader, the practical question is simple: *If a crisis of this magnitude hit your organization tomorrow, would you have the structure, relationships, and habits in place to respond with speed, clarity, and resilience—or would you be forced to improvise under fire?*

Chapter 1 Summary: The Vigilant Leader's Mindset

In this chapter, we:

- Distinguished **traditional** leadership—largely reactive and stability-focused—from **vigilant** leadership, which anticipates disruption and acts early.
- Defined vigilant leadership as a disciplined practice of **scanning, interpreting, deciding, and acting** in a fast-changing environment.

- Introduced the **Five Pillars of Vigilant Leadership**: Adaptability, Proactive Problem-Solving, Resilience, Ethical Decision-Making, and Continuous Learning.
- Identified **eight operational qualities**—such as strong relationships, effective communication, innovation, and data-driven decision-making—that bring vigilance to life in daily operations.
- Examined **real-world crises and case studies** (such as 9/11, COVID-19, Zoom, and Hertz) to illustrate the cost of missed signals and the power of decisive, proactive leadership.

The core message is simple: in today's world, vigilance is not a luxury or a personal preference. It is a requirement for any leader who intends to protect their people, stabilize their organization, and seize opportunities in the middle of volatility.

Leader Actions This Week

To translate Chapter 1 into action, choose at least **two** of the following and put them on your calendar:

- **Map your horizon.** Make a simple list of external forces that could impact your organization in the next 12–36 months (political, economic, technological, social). Highlight the top three that concern you most.
- **Run a "warning signals" conversation.** Ask a trusted group of front-line employees, "What are you worried about that leadership doesn't seem to see yet?" Listen without defending. Take notes.
- **Assess your five pillars.** For each pillar—Adaptability, Proactive Problem-Solving, Resilience, Ethical Decision-Making, Continuous Learning—rate yourself from 1–5.

Circle the lowest two and identify one behavior you can change this month.
- **Clarify one risk and one opportunity.** Identify a single emerging threat and a single emerging opportunity in your space. Write down what you will do about each in the next 30 days.
- **Block time for vigilance.** Schedule a recurring 30–60 minute "vigilance block" on your calendar each week dedicated to scanning, thinking ahead, and checking assumptions—not to answering email.

Questions for Your Team

Use these questions in a team meeting, one-on-ones, or your own journal:

1. **Where are we most vulnerable right now—and who is brave enough to say it out loud?**
2. **What early warning signs did we ignore in the past year?** (Customer complaints, market signals, missed opportunities, internal friction, etc.)
3. **If a serious disruption hit us tomorrow, what would fail first—and what does that reveal about our current level of vigilance?**

As you move into the next chapter, keep this principle in mind:

Vigilant leadership is not about predicting the future perfectly. It is about being less surprised than everyone else—and more prepared when the moment comes.

CHAPTER 2

THREAT IDENTIFICATION AND ASSESSMENT

"In the midst of chaos, there is also opportunity." – Sun Tzu

Modern organizations operate in a landscape where disruption is constant. Political shifts, economic shocks, social movements, and new technologies can reshape an industry faster than any annual plan. In this environment, leaders cannot afford to be surprised. Vigilant leadership starts with a clear understanding of the threats outside your walls and a disciplined approach to assessing them.

This chapter focuses on **threat identification and assessment**—the practical work of seeing what is coming, understanding what it means, and deciding how to respond. Where Chapter 1 established the mindset of a vigilant leader, Chapter 2 gives you tools to turn that mindset into concrete analysis.

2.1 Recognizing External Threats

No matter how strong your business plan is—or how successful you have been so far—external forces can undercut your position quickly. A new regulation, an unexpected election result, a shift in consumer values, or a disruptive technology can erode your advantage while you are busy executing last year's strategy.

Vigilant leaders do not wait for these forces to hit them. They **scan the horizon** regularly, looking for early signs of change. They ask hard questions:

- What political decisions could alter our operating environment?
- How might economic conditions squeeze our customers or our cash flow?
- What social or cultural trends are changing what people value and expect?
- Which technologies could either empower us—or make our current model obsolete?

To structure this work, we will use three proven tools:

- **PEST analysis** – to examine Political, Economic, Social, and Technological forces.
- **SWOT analysis** – to connect external realities with your internal Strengths, Weaknesses, Opportunities, and Threats.
- **Scenario planning** – to explore different possible futures and prepare for them in advance.

These tools are not new—but in the hands of a vigilant leader, they become more than academic exercises. They become part of a regular rhythm of scanning, thinking, and adjusting that keeps your organization ready for whatever comes next.

Next, we'll start with **PEST analysis**, a straightforward way to organize the external forces that could affect your business.

PEST Analysis

PEST analysis is a simple but powerful way to organize the external forces that can impact your organization. It helps you step out of day-to-day operations and look at the broader environment with discipline instead of guesswork.

PEST stands for:

- **Political**
- **Economic**
- **Social**
- **Technological**

Used well, PEST does three things for a vigilant leader:

1. Forces you to **scan beyond your industry** and pay attention to the country and world you operate in.
2. Helps you **separate noise from true signal** by grouping issues into clear categories.
3. Creates a shared language so your team can talk about external threats and opportunities without talking past each other.

You do not need a massive consulting project to use PEST. You need a whiteboard, a small group of sharp people, and the discipline to ask direct questions about what could affect your mission.

Political Factors

Political factors include government actions and policies that can help or hurt your organization. For a U.S.-based or U.S.-focused leader, this means paying close attention to:

- Laws and regulations that affect your industry
- Tax and labor policy changes
- Trade policy and tariffs

- National security decisions that affect supply chains or technology
- Shifts in enforcement priorities (what regulators actually focus on)

Key questions for a vigilant leader:

- What new or proposed laws could increase our costs, limit our operations, or open new doors?
- Are there upcoming elections or policy debates that could reshape our market or workforce?
- Where are we exposed if enforcement becomes stricter—or if it becomes looser and competitors cut corners?
- Which relationships (industry groups, legal counsel, local officials) do we need in place before a political shock hits?

Political changes are not something you control, but they are absolutely something you must anticipate. Ignoring them is not neutrality; it is vulnerability.

Economic Factors

Economic factors deal with the health and direction of the broader economy and your specific markets. They directly influence your customers' ability to spend and your own cost structure.

Consider:

- Interest rates and access to capital
- Inflation and input costs
- Employment levels and wage pressures
- Currency fluctuations (if you operate globally)
- Overall consumer and business confidence

Key questions:

- If interest rates rise or stay high, how does that affect our debt, expansion plans, and customer spending?
- How sensitive is our business to inflation in materials, shipping, or labor?
- Are our key customers in sectors that are growing, flat, or contracting?
- Do we have enough financial margin to handle a slowdown, or are we operating on the edge?

Vigilant leaders do not guess about economic exposure; they map it and plan for it.

Social Factors

Social factors include cultural values, demographics, and public attitudes that shape how people live, work, and buy. These changes are often slower than technology shifts, but they are just as powerful.

Examples:

- Demographic trends (aging population, generational shifts)
- Attitudes toward work, flexibility, and benefits
- Expectations around health, safety, and well-being
- Shifts in trust toward institutions, brands, or industries
- Lifestyle changes that affect where and how people spend time and money

Key questions:

- How are our core customers changing in age, values, or expectations?
- Are there emerging expectations around service, responsiveness, or flexibility that we are ignoring?
- How does the public perceive our industry—and what would it take to lose or regain trust?

- Are there groups we are unintentionally alienating or overlooking?

Vigilant leaders pay attention to social undercurrents because those undercurrents become tomorrow's "sudden" market changes.

Technological Factors

Technological factors include new tools, platforms, and capabilities that can either empower your organization or make your current model obsolete.

This covers:

- Automation and AI
- Digital platforms and communication tools
- Cybersecurity risks
- New manufacturing or logistics technologies
- Data and analytics capabilities

Key questions:

- What technologies could **dramatically lower costs** or **improve speed and quality** if we adopted them early?
- What technologies could **undermine our current advantage** if a competitor adopted them first?
- Where are we vulnerable to cyberattacks, data loss, or systems failure?
- Do we have the right people and partners to evaluate and implement new tech, or are we guessing?

Technology is not neutral. It either gives you leverage—or gives someone else leverage over you.

Putting PEST into Practice

A PEST analysis does not have to be complicated:

1. Gather a small group of leaders and front-line voices.
2. Create four columns: Political, Economic, Social, Technological.
3. Spend 30–60 minutes listing anything in each category that could significantly affect your organization in the next 12–36 months.
4. Highlight the **top three to five items** across all four categories.
5. For each of those, ask: *What can we do now to prepare, protect, or position ourselves?*

That simple exercise, repeated quarterly or even twice a year, will put you ahead of leaders who only think about the external environment when a crisis arrives.

Next, we'll connect this external view to your internal reality by using **SWOT analysis** to understand how your strengths and weaknesses interact with the opportunities and threats you've identified.

SWOT Analysis

Once you've used PEST to map the external environment, the next step is to connect that outside reality to your **internal** reality. That is where **SWOT analysis** comes in.

SWOT stands for:

- **Strengths**
- **Weaknesses**

- **Opportunities**
- **Threats**

Used well, SWOT helps a vigilant leader answer a simple question:

Given the world we're operating in, how prepared are we—really?

PEST shows you the landscape. SWOT shows you how fit you are to move through it.

Why SWOT Still Matters

SWOT is a familiar tool, and because of that, many leaders treat it as a checkbox exercise for planning retreats. Vigilant leaders use it differently. They:

- Tie SWOT directly to the **specific political, economic, social, and technological forces** identified in their PEST.
- Force honest discussion about **where they are strong and where they are exposed**, instead of producing a feel-good list.
- Use SWOT to **prioritize action**, not just to fill slides.

The goal is not a pretty matrix. The goal is a clear, shared view of where you can win, where you are vulnerable, and where disciplined action is required.

Building a Vigilant SWOT

Start with a simple four-quadrant grid on a whiteboard or digital board:

Strengths | Weaknesses
Opportunities | Threats

Then work through each quadrant with focus.

Strengths

Strengths are internal capabilities that give you an advantage.

They might include:

- A strong, loyal customer base
- A trusted brand and reputation
- Operational excellence in a key area (speed, quality, safety)
- A highly skilled or highly committed team
- Superior data, systems, or processes

Key questions:

- What do we consistently do better than our competitors?
- Where do our customers say we add the most value?
- Which capabilities would be hardest for others to copy quickly?

Vigilant leaders are specific here. "We have great people" is not enough. Name the exact strengths that matter in your current environment.

Weaknesses

Weaknesses are internal limitations that reduce your ability to compete or respond.

These might include:

- Overdependence on one major customer, supplier, or product
- Outdated systems, facilities, or technology

- Gaps in skills, leadership, or bench strength
- Slow decision-making or bureaucratic processes
- Poor data quality or inconsistent execution

Key questions:

- Where do we consistently fall short or drop the ball?
- What do our best people complain about privately?
- If a competitor were analyzing us, what would they see as obvious vulnerabilities?

Vigilant leaders do not sugarcoat weaknesses. They know that **denied weaknesses become tomorrow's crises**.

Opportunities

Opportunities are external conditions you can use to your advantage.

To stay grounded, pull directly from your **PEST analysis** and ask:

- Which political decisions, policy changes, or public investments could favor our strategy?
- Are there economic shifts (new markets, reshoring, regional growth) we can leverage?
- Are social trends moving in a direction that aligns with our strengths and values?
- Which technologies could help us increase efficiency, improve service, or open new lines of business?

Key questions:

- Where can we use our existing strengths to solve emerging problems better than others?
- What customer needs are not being met—or not being met well—by our competitors?

- Where are our competitors slow, arrogant, or distracted?

Opportunities should not be wishful thinking; they should be **specific openings in a real environment**.

Threats

Threats are external forces that could damage your position, erode your margins, or undermine your mission.

Again, pull from your PEST:

- Political or regulatory changes that increase costs or restrict operations
- Economic downturns, inflation, or interest-rate pressures that squeeze you or your customers
- Social shifts that reduce trust in your industry or change what people value
- Technologies that could replace your product, your service, or your role in the value chain

Key questions:

- What could realistically hurt us in the next 12–36 months if we do nothing?
- Where are we exposed to decisions made by others (government, large customers, key partners)?
- What new players, models, or technologies could make us less relevant?

Vigilant leaders neither panic nor downplay threats. They **name them clearly** and plan accordingly.

Common Mistakes to Avoid

When running SWOT, watch out for these traps:

- **Laundry lists:** Long, vague lists with no prioritization. Focus on what truly matters.
- **Biased optimism:** Overemphasizing strengths and opportunities while minimizing weaknesses and threats.
- **No connection to PEST:** Listing generic items that ignore the real external environment.
- **No follow-through:** Completing the matrix, then filing it away and changing nothing.

A sloppy SWOT is worse than no SWOT, because it creates an illusion of diligence without the substance.

From SWOT to Action

The real power of SWOT comes from what you do afterward. Once your grid is filled, ask your team to identify a few key strategic moves:

- **Use Strengths to capture Opportunities.**
    - Where can we lean on our best capabilities to take advantage of what's changing?
- **Use Strengths to counter Threats.**
    - Which strengths can we deploy to blunt or neutralize the most serious threats?
- **Reduce Weaknesses that make Threats more dangerous.**
    - Which weaknesses must we address now because they will make external threats far more costly if we ignore them?
- **Avoid chasing Opportunities that expose Weaknesses.**
    - Are there tempting opportunities we should decline because we are not yet ready to execute them well?

Finally, narrow the list. Choose **three to five concrete actions** that will:

1. Strengthen one or two key capabilities,
2. Reduce one or two serious vulnerabilities, and
3. Position you better against the most critical external forces.

Assign owners, deadlines, and metrics. If your SWOT does not produce next steps with names and dates, you haven't finished the exercise.

Next, we'll look at **scenario planning**—a practical way to explore different possible futures and pressure-test your strategies against them before they become reality.

Scenario Planning

PEST helps you understand the environment. SWOT helps you understand your position in that environment. **Scenario planning** helps you prepare for how that environment might actually play out.

You cannot predict the future with precision—but you also cannot afford to be surprised by every turn. Scenario planning gives vigilant leaders a disciplined way to explore different plausible futures and test how ready they are for each.

Think of it as **wargaming for your organization**: you ask, "If the world goes this way, what happens to us—and what do we do now so we're not scrambling later?"

Why Scenario Planning Matters

In a volatile world, leaders who plan only for the "most likely" outcome end up exposed when reality bends in another direction. Scenario planning:

- Prevents overconfidence in a single forecast.
- Reveals where your strategies are fragile or overdependent on one assumption.
- Forces you to think in **options**, not just linear plans.
- Makes it easier to move quickly when conditions change, because you have already thought through alternatives.

Vigilant leaders do not wait for certainty; they prepare for a range of plausible conditions.

A Simple Scenario Planning Process

You do not need a thick binder or a consulting firm to do this. A focused half-day with the right people can be powerful.

Step 1: Identify Key Uncertainties

From your PEST and SWOT work, ask:

- What are the **two or three biggest uncertainties** that could significantly affect us in the next 1–3 years?
    - Examples: pace of economic recovery, regulatory changes, adoption of a new technology, key partner stability, geopolitical tensions.

Write them clearly. These are the variables your scenarios will revolve around.

Step 2: Define a Small Set of Plausible Futures

Pick **3–4 scenarios**, not 10. Each should be:

- Plausible (not science fiction)
- Different enough to matter
- Relevant to your organization

For example, for a U.S.-based company you might define:

1. **Stable but Tight** – Slow growth, moderate inflation, cautious customers, no major policy shocks.
2. **Regulation Shock** – New regulations or compliance burdens significantly increase your operating costs.
3. **Tech Disruption** – A new technology changes how customers expect to buy or use services in your space.
4. **Crisis and Reset** – A major event (economic downturn, cyberattack, supply disruption) forces sudden cuts and rapid restructuring.

You don't need to attach probabilities. The question is: *If this happened, how ready would we be?*

Step 3: Stress-Test Your Strategy

For each scenario, ask:

- How would this future affect our customers?
- How would it hit our revenue, costs, and operations?
- Which of our **strengths** become more valuable—and which **weaknesses** become dangerous?
- What parts of our current strategy still work, and what breaks?

Capture the answers in simple bullets under each scenario. You're not writing a novel; you're mapping pressure points.

Step 4: Decide on No-Regrets Moves and Contingent Options

From your analysis, identify:

- **No-regrets moves** – Actions that make sense in almost every scenario.

- - Example: strengthening cash reserves, investing in data and cybersecurity, cross-training key roles, improving customer insight.
- **Contingent options** – Moves you won't execute yet, but you will prepare for.
  - Example: if regulation shocks hit, you're ready to consolidate locations; if tech disruption accelerates, you're ready to fast-track a digital offering.

Document these clearly:

- What will we do now (no-regrets)?
- What will we **prepare** to do if certain signals appear (contingent)?
- Who owns monitoring those signals, and how often will we review them?

That discipline is what turns scenario planning from an intellectual exercise into a practical vigilance tool.

A Brief Example

Imagine you lead a mid-sized service company heavily dependent on one major corporate client.

From PEST and SWOT, you've identified:

- Economic uncertainty and rising interest rates
- Increasing use of AI tools in your industry
- A weakness: overdependence on the top client

You run three scenarios:

1. **Client Stays Strong, Market Stable** – Status quo holds, mild economic pressure.

2. **Client Cuts Back** – Your largest client reduces spending by 30% due to cost-cutting.
3. **AI Adoption Accelerates** – Your services are partially replaced or expected to be enhanced by AI.

You might discover:

- In Scenario 2, your revenue drops sharply and your lack of diversification becomes a serious threat.
- In Scenario 3, your offering looks dated unless you integrate AI into your process.

No-regrets moves might include:

- Expanding your client base now, even if it lowers short-term margins.
- Building or partnering to add AI-enhanced services before customers demand them.

Contingent options might include:

- A pre-defined cost-control plan you only trigger if Scenario 2 signs appear.
- An accelerated hiring or partnership plan if Scenario 3 signals show up faster than expected.

None of this requires a crystal ball; it requires structured imagination backed by discipline.

Common Pitfalls in Scenario Planning

Avoid these traps:

- **Focusing only on best-case or worst-case.** You need a few *realistic* middle-path scenarios, not just extremes.

- **Creating scenarios you secretly hope for.** This becomes fantasy, not planning.
- **Treating scenarios as predictions.** They are tools for preparation, not bets.
- **No follow-up.** Running a workshop, then never revisiting the scenarios or their signals.

Vigilant leaders tie scenario planning to their calendar. They review key assumptions quarterly or at major decision points and adjust when signs point toward one scenario becoming more likely.

Used together, **PEST, SWOT, and scenario planning** give you a structured way to:

- See the external environment clearly,
- Understand your real position within it, and
- Prepare for multiple plausible futures instead of gambling on one.

2.2 Internal Threats: Culture, Systems, and Leadership

So far, we have focused on external forces—political, economic, social, and technological shifts—and how to analyze them using PEST, SWOT, and scenario planning. But many of the most dangerous threats to an organization don't come from the outside at all.

They come from **within**.

A vigilant leader understands that culture, systems, and leadership behavior can quietly become internal threats that magnify every external shock. If you ignore them, no amount of clever analysis will save you when pressure hits.

We'll look at three internal threat zones:

- Culture
- Systems and processes
- Leadership behavior

Culture: Your Early Warning System—or Your Blindfold

Culture is what people really believe and do when no one is watching. It determines whether front-line employees speak up or stay silent, whether bad news travels quickly or gets buried, and whether teams pull together or protect their own turf.

Signals of a culture that undermines vigilance:

- **Fear of speaking up.** People worry about being punished, ignored, or labeled "negative" for raising concerns.
- **Complacency.** "We've always done it this way" is treated as a defense, not a warning sign.
- **Silo mentality.** Departments guard information instead of sharing it. Threats and opportunities are seen as "their problem" or "not my job."
- **Blame culture.** When something goes wrong, the first impulse is to find a scapegoat instead of understanding the system failure.

In that environment, weak signals never reach leadership until they become full-blown crises.

Vigilant leaders build a different culture:

- They **invite honest feedback**, especially from the front lines.
- They **reward early warning**, not just heroic firefighting.
- They **respond to bad news with questions and action**, not anger and denial.

- They **model accountability**, taking responsibility for decisions rather than pushing blame downward.

A practical question: *If there were a serious brewing problem in your organization right now, how confident are you that you would hear about it early?*

Systems and Processes: Quiet Weak Points

Even with good people and decent culture, outdated or poorly designed systems can create hidden vulnerabilities:

- Manual processes that depend on one or two "indispensable" individuals
- Critical data spread across disconnected spreadsheets and tools
- No clear owner for key risks (cybersecurity, vendor reliability, safety, compliance)
- Metrics that reward short-term results while ignoring long-term exposure

These weaknesses often stay invisible until something breaks—someone leaves, a system fails, a vendor collapses, or a minor issue scales rapidly.

Vigilant leaders:

- Identify **single points of failure** and build backups.
- Standardize and document critical processes.
- Ensure that **key risks have named owners** with real authority.
- Align metrics so that people are rewarded not only for results, but also for responsible, resilient practices.

A practical question: *Where are we relying on habit, heroics, or memory instead of clear, resilient systems?*

Leadership Behavior: The Biggest Internal Threat

Finally, the most powerful internal threat is leadership behavior itself.

Even smart, experienced leaders can undermine vigilance when they:

- Dismiss uncomfortable information because it conflicts with their assumptions
- Surround themselves with people who tell them what they want to hear
- Delay decisions hoping for perfect certainty
- Change direction constantly, exhausting the team and blurring priorities
- Treat criticism or questioning as disloyalty

When this happens, the organization learns a dangerous lesson: **it is safer to stay quiet and deliver what the boss expects than to tell the truth.** At that point, the formal tools of vigilance (PEST, SWOT, scenarios) become hollow rituals. People stop sharing what they really see.

Vigilant leaders, by contrast:

- Ask direct questions like, "What am I missing?" and "What bad news should I know sooner?"
- Publicly **thank people who raise hard issues**, even when those issues create more work.
- Make timely decisions, then adjust as new information appears—instead of hiding behind endless analysis.
- Admit when they were wrong and change course without drama.

- Hold themselves and others accountable with the same standards.

A practical question: *If your team were completely honest, would they say your behavior makes it easier—or harder—for them to be vigilant?*

Reality Check

At this point in the chapter, you have three lenses:

- **PEST** to scan the environment
- **SWOT** to evaluate your position
- **Scenario planning** to explore plausible futures

Now add this fourth lens: **internal threats** rooted in culture, systems, and leadership behavior.

Without that reality check, you can be technically sophisticated and still strategically blind.

Before moving on, take a moment and write down:

1. One cultural issue that could block early warning in your organization.
2. One system or process that feels more fragile than it should.
3. One leadership habit of your own that could discourage honest input.

These are not weaknesses to be ashamed of; they are opportunities to strengthen your vigilance from the inside out.

Chapter 2 Summary: Seeing the Whole Playing Field

In Chapter 2, we moved from mindset to method. You learned how to use a set of practical tools to identify and assess threats before they overwhelm you.

We:

- Introduced **PEST analysis** as a way to scan political, economic, social, and technological forces shaping your environment.
- Used **SWOT analysis** to connect those external forces to your internal strengths and weaknesses.
- Applied **scenario planning** to explore multiple plausible futures and identify "no-regrets" moves and contingent options.
- Examined **internal threats** in culture, systems, and leadership behavior that can undermine vigilance from within.

The message is straightforward: vigilant leaders see both **outside-in** and **inside-out**. They understand the landscape, their own condition, and the range of futures they may face—and they prepare accordingly.

Leader Actions This Week

Choose at least **two** of these actions and put them on your calendar:

- **Run a quick PEST scan.** With a small team, spend 30–45 minutes listing key political, economic, social, and technological factors that could affect your organization in the next 1–3 years. Highlight the top three.

- **Do a focused SWOT.** Using your PEST output, create a one-page SWOT that honestly names your top strengths, weaknesses, opportunities, and threats. Don't over-polish it.
- **Define three scenarios.** Draft three simple, plausible future scenarios (e.g., regulation shock, economic slowdown, tech disruption) and write 5–10 bullet points for how each would impact your organization.
- **Identify one internal threat.** Ask a few trusted people, "What internal habit, system, or cultural issue worries you the most?" Listen, and pick one to address.
- **Assign signal-watchers.** For your top two external threats, assign a specific person to monitor key indicators (legislation, economic data, technology moves, competitor activity) and report regularly.

Questions for Your Team

Use these in a leadership meeting, strategy session, or off-site:

1. **If we were a competitor, where would we attack us first?**
2. **Which external threat do we talk about the most—and which one do we avoid because it makes us uncomfortable?**
3. **Where in our culture or systems are we most likely to miss early warning signs? What will we do about it?**

As you move into the next chapter, remember:

Vigilance is not paranoia. It is disciplined awareness, paired with the courage to act before circumstances force your hand.

CHAPTER 3

INDUSTRY-SPECIFIC FORESIGHT STRATEGIES

"The only thing more dangerous than not seeing the future is believing it's predictable."
— Patrick Lencioni

Every industry plays by its own rules. Healthcare, finance, manufacturing, technology, fitness, education—each has its own regulators, risk profile, culture, and pace of change. Vigilant leadership is not a generic skill you practice in a vacuum. It must be **anchored in the realities of your sector**.

Disruptive technologies, shifting regulations, changing customer expectations, and geopolitical volatility are reshaping markets faster than ever. Some leaders treat this as background noise. Vigilant leaders treat it as their job description.

In this chapter, we focus on **industry-specific foresight**—how to apply the principles from Chapters 1 and 2 to the actual arena you compete in. You will:

- Learn how to read the dynamics of your industry more clearly.
- Tailor your leadership approach to your sector instead of relying on generic advice.
- See how leaders in different fields have used vigilance to gain an edge—or lost it by ignoring signals.

The goal is simple: to help you become the leader in your industry who sees change coming and is ready for it.

3.1 Adapting Vigilance to Industries

Understanding Industry Dynamics

Every industry is shaped by a unique mix of forces:

- In **healthcare**, regulation, safety, ethics, and technology collide in ways that directly impact human lives.
- In **finance**, risk, regulation, and market psychology can move billions of dollars in a day.
- In **technology**, speed of innovation and disruption is relentless.
- In **hospitality and service sectors**, brand, trust, and guest experience can swing on a single viral incident.

The specifics change, but the principle is the same: **you cannot lead vigilantly if you don't understand the rules, pressures, and players in your arena.**

Vigilant leaders make it their business to know:

- Who the major players and emerging disruptors are.
- How money really moves in their industry.
- Which regulators, standards, and policies matter.
- What customers value now—and what they are starting to value next.

They are students of their industry, not just occupants of a role.

Tailoring Leadership Strategies

The days when deep experience in a single company was enough are over. Long tenure can still be an asset—but only if you combine it with **deliberate exposure to different parts of the value chain and, in many cases, other organizations.**

Vigilant leaders:

- Get out of their lane and learn how other departments, partners, and competitors operate.
- Study different business models within their industry—traditional players, low-cost entrants, premium brands, digital-first startups.
- Look for patterns and pressure points that most people ignore because they are busy with day-to-day demands.

In some careers, that might mean:

- Moving between roles in **operations, strategy, and customer-facing functions** to see the whole picture.
- Switching companies or divisions to understand different segments of the industry.
- Serving on cross-industry committees, councils, or boards that give visibility into broader trends.

The more contexts you've experienced, the better your **strategic vision** becomes. Vigilance is easier when you've seen the same pattern from multiple angles.

Where to Start?

Information is everywhere. The problem is not access—it's discipline.

Many leaders "skim" their industry:

- Skimming a few headlines.
- Glancing at quarterly reports.
- Reacting to rumors or social media spikes.

Vigilant leaders build a **simple, repeatable routine** instead of relying on random exposure:

- Subscribe to a short, high-quality list of **industry journals, newsletters, or briefings**.
- Follow key **regulators, analysts, and serious operators** (not just influencers) who actually move the sector.
- Attend **one or two strategic conferences or forums** a year where serious people discuss what's coming, not just what already happened.
- Schedule a recurring monthly or quarterly **"industry scan" block** where you—and ideally a small team—review what has changed and what it means.

The key is consistency. A leader who spends one focused hour a month scanning with intent will be far more vigilant than a leader who occasionally binge-reads when a crisis hits.

Cultivating Industry Expertise

Continuous learning and professional development are not optional if you intend to lead at a high level in your industry.

Vigilant leaders:

- Pursue **relevant certifications, advanced training, or executive education** tied directly to their sector.
- Participate in **industry associations, standards groups, and think tanks** where future trends are debated and shaped.

- Build **trusted relationships** with peers and mentors in other organizations who will share honest insights, not just marketing spin.
- Make time to **mentor others**, because teaching forces you to clarify your own understanding.

Over time, this positions you not just as a manager, but as a **trusted voice** in your field—a person others look to when they want to understand what's really going on and what might come next.

Adapting Vigilant Leadership to Specific Industries

While the core principles of vigilant leadership are universal, their application varies by industry. Consider just a few examples:

- **Healthcare**
    - Must balance innovation with patient safety and strict regulatory compliance.
    - Vigilant leaders track policy shifts, technology advances (telemedicine, AI diagnostics), and public expectations about access and ethics.
- **Financial Services**
    - Operates under intense regulatory scrutiny and real-time market risk.
    - Vigilant leaders invest heavily in risk management, compliance, and technology that allows them to see exposure early and act quickly.
- **Technology and Digital Platforms**
    - Face constant disruption and short product cycles.
    - Vigilant leaders watch emerging technologies, platform shifts, data-privacy rules, and competitive moves with unusual intensity.
- **Fitness and Wellness**

- Navigate trends, safety concerns, evolving client expectations, and legal/reputational risk.
- Vigilant leaders monitor changes in consumer behavior, safety standards, and the impact of AI, wearables, and remote coaching.

Your task as a vigilant leader is to:

1. **Name the specific forces** that shape your industry.
2. **Identify the few that matter most** to your organization.
3. **Deliberately align your leadership practices**—communication, hiring, investment, partnerships—around those realities.

The rest of this chapter will show how leaders in different sectors have done this in practice and how you can borrow, adapt, and apply those lessons to your own environment.

3.2 Industry Case Studies: Foresight in Action

Theory is cheap. Vigilant leadership earns its worth when it shows up in real decisions, under real pressure, in specific industries. The following brief case studies illustrate how foresight plays out in different arenas—and what happens when it doesn't.

Use them as patterns, not scripts. Your job is to ask, "What is the version of this in *my* world?"

Case Study: Amazon – Logistics as Strategic Foresight

(Retail / Logistics / Technology)

Amazon did not become a dominant player by accident or by focusing only on quarterly numbers. From the beginning, leadership treated **logistics, data, and customer obsession** as strategic weapons.

Foresight moves included:

- Aggressively reinvesting profits into **fulfillment centers**, last-mile delivery, and technology infrastructure long before competitors took e-commerce seriously.
- Using data from millions of transactions to anticipate demand, optimize inventory, and shorten delivery times.
- Expanding into web services (AWS) when most retailers were still figuring out email marketing.

Vigilance lessons:

- They read the trajectory of **consumer behavior and technology** early and bet on it.
- They treated infrastructure as a long-term advantage, not a cost to be minimized.
- They used data to see around corners while others were guessing.

Your question: *What "infrastructure" in my industry—physical, digital, or relational—could become a long-term advantage if I invest before everyone else?*

Case Study: JPMorgan Chase – Risk Vigilance in Financial Services

(Banking / Risk / Regulation)

Financial services lives and dies on risk management. JPMorgan Chase has not been perfect—but it has consistently treated **risk,**

regulation, and capital strength as strategic priorities, not back-office chores.

Foresight moves include:

- Building strong **risk frameworks and stress-testing practices** that consider multiple economic scenarios.
- Maintaining a focus on **capital and liquidity** so the bank can absorb shocks and stay in the fight when conditions tighten.
- Investing heavily in **cybersecurity and digital capabilities**, recognizing that future attacks and disruptions will be digital, not just financial.

Vigilance lessons:

- They understand that in their industry, **staying power is a competitive advantage**.
- They plan for downturns and regulatory shifts long before they hit.
- They treat cybersecurity and operational resilience as non-negotiable.

Your question: *In my world, what form does "capital and resilience" take—and am I building it on purpose or hoping I won't need it?*

Case Study: A National Fitness Chain – Safety, Reputation, and Legal Foresight

(Health / Fitness / Liability)

Consider a large fitness chain that built its brand on low prices and 24-hour access. Membership growth was strong, but leadership treated **safety, trainer conduct, and legal exposure** as an afterthought. Background checks were inconsistent, training on boundaries and appropriate touch was minimal, and incident reporting was informal.

Over time:

- Complaints about inappropriate behavior and poor supervision began to surface.
- Social media posts and local news stories drew attention to injuries and alleged misconduct.
- Lawsuits followed, insurance costs climbed, and the brand's "welcoming" reputation took a hit.

The leadership team had focused on **sales and expansion**, but not on the downstream risk created by poor hiring, weak policies, and inconsistent enforcement of standards. They were reacting to each incident instead of building a system to prevent them.

Vigilance lessons:

- In high-contact industries, **safety and boundaries are business-critical**, not "HR issues."
- A few unchecked incidents can snowball into major legal, financial, and reputational damage.
- Proactive policies, training, supervision, and enforcement are cheaper than crisis management.

Your question: *Where in my organization could a pattern of small, tolerated issues quietly turn into a reputational or legal crisis?*

Case Study: Jack Ma and Alibaba – Political Risk and the Limits of Foresight

(Global Platforms / Political Risk)

Jack Ma and Alibaba built one of the world's most powerful e-commerce and financial-technology ecosystems. From a pure business perspective, their foresight was impressive: they anticipated the growth of online commerce in China, built powerful digital platforms, and expanded rapidly.

But Alibaba's environment was not a free market in the American sense. It operated within a **state-controlled system** with different rules and a different tolerance for outspoken business leaders. When Jack Ma publicly criticized elements of the Chinese regulatory and financial system, political risk surfaced quickly and decisively. Regulatory action halted Ant Group's massive IPO and tightened control over key parts of the business.

Vigilance lessons:

- Industry foresight is not enough if you **misread the political environment** you operate in.
- The rules of the game are not the same in every country or system.
- Leaders must understand not only markets and technology, but also the **limits of what is tolerated** by those in power.

Your question: *What political or regulatory red lines exist in my environment—and am I clear-eyed about them, or assuming the rules will bend for me?*

Case Study: IBM Under Ginni Rometty – Reinventing a Legacy Player

(Technology / Services / Reinvention)

IBM began as a hardware giant. By the time Ginni Rometty took the helm as CEO, the company faced intense pressure from cloud providers, new software models, and changing customer expectations.

Foresight moves included:

- Continuing the shift from **hardware to higher-margin services, consulting, analytics, and cloud.**
- Investing in emerging areas like **AI and security**, knowing that clients would need help navigating complexity, not just buying machines.
- Exiting or de-emphasizing businesses that no longer fit the future IBM was building.

Results were mixed and the journey was far from smooth, but the core instinct was right: a legacy player cannot survive by defending its past; it must **choose what to become next.**

Vigilance lessons:

- Reinvention is messy, but **fighting the future is fatal**.
- Leaders must make tough calls about where to double down and where to let go.
- It is better to start the shift while you still have strength than to wait until decline forces desperate measures.

Your question: *What part of our business am I defending mainly because it's familiar—not because it's truly part of our future?*

3.3 The Industry Foresight Playbook

You've seen how vigilance plays out in different sectors. Now we'll turn that into a simple, repeatable **Industry Foresight Playbook** you can use in your own organization.

You don't need all of this on day one. Start where you are, but be honest about where you need to go.

1. Define Your Arena Clearly

- What industry are you *actually* in?
- What problems do you really solve, and for whom?
- Who are your true competitors and substitutes (including digital or "do nothing" options)?

2. Build a Focused Signal Panel

- Identify a short list of **data sources, reports, and briefings** that truly matter.
- Include: regulators, key competitors, trade groups, serious analysts, and customer feedback sources.
- Cut the noise; keep what helps you see change early.

3. Run Regular Industry PEST Scans

- Quarterly or semi-annually, run a PEST specifically for **your industry**, not just the general economy.
- Ask: What has changed politically, economically, socially, and technologically since our last scan?

4. Maintain a Competitor and Disruptor Map

- Track incumbents, low-cost entrants, premium niche players, and digital-first challengers.
- Watch not only what they sell, but **how** they deliver, price, and position themselves.

5. Listen Deeply to Customers

- Use surveys, interviews, front-line feedback, and social listening to track what customers value *now* and what frustrates them.
- Look for early signs that expectations are rising or shifting.

6. Establish a Risk and Opportunity Radar

- Identify your top **regulatory, legal, reputational, tech, and supply chain** risks.
- Pair each with potential **opportunities** that could emerge from change (new markets, new needs, new partnerships).

7. Create a Small Foresight Council

- Assemble a cross-functional group (e.g., operations, finance, tech, HR, customer-facing teams) that meets regularly to review signals.
- Keep it small, serious, and action-oriented.

8. Use Scenario Planning Annually

- Once a year, run a focused scenario exercise: 3–4 plausible futures for your industry.
- Identify no-regrets moves and contingent options, as in Chapter 2.

9. Align Budget and Investment to Foresight

- Put real money behind what your foresight reveals.
- Invest in capabilities, systems, and people that will matter in your likely futures—not just what made sense five years ago.

10. Turn Foresight into Simple Narratives

- Craft 1–2 clear internal narratives: "Here's where our industry is headed; here's how we intend to win."

- Use plain language; your people should be able to repeat it.

11. Communicate and Cascade

- Share key insights and implications with managers and front-line teams.
- Connect strategy to daily decisions, not just slide decks.

12. Track a Short List of Leading Indicators

- Identify a **small set of metrics** that tend to move before major shifts (e.g., certain customer behaviors, regulatory milestones, tech adoption rates).
- Review them regularly.

13. Review and Adjust

- At least twice a year, revisit your foresight assumptions.
- What did we get right? What changed faster or slower than expected?
- Adjust plans accordingly.

14. Build Bench Strength with Industry Breadth

- Develop future leaders who have worked in more than one function or business line.
- Give high-potential people assignments that broaden their view of the industry.

15. Maintain Your Own Discipline

- Protect time on your calendar for **reading, thinking, and relationship-building** beyond your company's walls.
- As a leader, your personal vigilance sets the tone for the entire organization.

Chapter 3 Summary: Becoming a Student of Your Industry

In this chapter, you:

- Learned why **vigilance must be anchored in the specific realities of your industry**, not just generic leadership theory.
- Saw how different sectors—retail, finance, fitness, global platforms, and technology—reward or punish leaders based on their foresight.
- Built an **Industry Foresight Playbook** you can adapt to your own arena.

The core idea: **you cannot lead well in an industry you don't truly study.** Vigilant leaders make it their business to understand the forces, players, and future trajectories of their field—and they act before change turns into crisis.

Leader Actions This Week

Pick at least **two**:

- **Name your top 3 industry forces.** Write down the three external forces you believe will most shape your industry in the next 3–5 years. Share them with your team and ask if they agree.
- **Build a signal list.** Create or refine a short list of must-read sources (regulators, analysts, trade groups, serious operators) and schedule 30 minutes per week to review them.
- **Map your competitors and disruptors.** Sketch a simple map of incumbents, low-cost players, premium brands, and digital disruptors. Mark who worries you most—and why.

- **Start a mini foresight council.** Invite 3–5 sharp people from different parts of your organization to meet quarterly to discuss industry trends and what they mean for you.
- **Identify one no-regrets investment.** Based on what you already know about your industry's future, choose one capability, system, or relationship to strengthen in the next 90 days.

Questions for Your Team

Use these in a leadership meeting, off-site, or strategy session:

1. **If our industry changes in the way we *expect*, are we ahead of the curve—or barely keeping pace?**
2. **What recent move by a competitor or disruptor surprised us—and why didn't we see it coming?**
3. **If we had to bet our own savings on one major shift in our industry over the next three years, what would it be—and how are we preparing for it now?**

With Chapters 1–3, you now have:

- A **mindset** (vigilant leadership),
- A **set of tools** (PEST, SWOT, scenarios, internal threat checks), and
- An **industry lens** to anchor them in reality.

CHAPTER 4

AI IN BUSINESS FORESIGHT

Artificial intelligence is not a gimmick or a toy. Used well, it is a **force multiplier** for vigilant leaders. It helps you see patterns faster, scan more information than any human team can handle on its own, and test decisions before you commit real dollars.

Used poorly, AI becomes another shiny object that burns cash, confuses your team, and distracts you from the basics.

This chapter will not turn you into a data scientist. It will show you, as a leader, **how to think about AI as a strategic asset**:

- Where AI can sharpen foresight and decision-making
- How real organizations are using it to gain an advantage
- What questions you should be asking before you invest
- How AI supports—not replaces—your Five Pillars of Vigilant Leadership

---

4.1 Why AI Matters for Vigilant Leaders

Vigilant leadership is about **seeing sooner, deciding better, and acting faster** than your competitors.

AI strengthens that in three major ways:

1. **Data at scale**
   AI can sift through millions of data points—customer behavior, market signals, operational data—and surface patterns no human will ever see on a spreadsheet.
2. **Faster pattern recognition**
   Properly trained models detect anomalies, trends, and correlations early: fraud attempts, demand shifts, emerging risks, maintenance problems, and more.
3. **Better "what if" analysis**
   AI-powered forecasting and simulation tools let you test scenarios—pricing changes, inventory strategies, capacity planning—before you move.

But AI does not lead. **People lead.**

Your job as a vigilant leader is to:

- Decide where AI can genuinely support your mission
- Insist on clear business outcomes, not buzzwords
- Put guardrails around data, ethics, and security
- Develop your people so they can use AI wisely

4.2 Case Studies: AI-Enabled Vigilance in Action

Retail: Seeing Demand Before It Hits the Shelf

A major retailer with thousands of locations faces a basic but brutal challenge: if they can't predict demand, they either lose sales to empty shelves or lose money to excess inventory.

By implementing **AI-driven predictive analytics**, leadership pulls together:

- Historical sales

- Seasonality and holidays
- Local events and promotions
- Weather patterns and regional trends

The system generates more accurate store-level forecasts, which in turn:

- Reduces out-of-stock incidents
- Cuts waste and carrying costs
- Improves product availability and customer satisfaction

Vigilance lesson:
Leadership didn't use AI for the sake of "innovation theater." They targeted a core problem—inventory accuracy—that directly affects profit, customer trust, and competitive advantage. AI amplified a disciplined strategy; it did not substitute for one.

Vigilant Leadership 1.0 Manuscr...

Ask yourself: *Where in my business does poor prediction quietly cost us real money and goodwill?*

Financial Services: Real-Time Fraud Detection

In the financial sector, fraud is not just a nuisance—it is an existential threat to trust.

Traditional rule-based systems look for known patterns: if a transaction violates a rule, it gets flagged. Criminals adapt quickly, and those static rules fall behind.

By deploying **AI-based fraud detection**, a leading financial institution:

- Analyzes transaction patterns in real time

VIGILANT LEADERSHIP

- Uses machine learning to spot unusual behavior, not just known schemes
- Applies natural language processing to unstructured data (notes, messages, claims) to spot hidden signals

The result: more fraud caught sooner, fewer legitimate transactions blocked, and stronger confidence from customers and regulators.

Vigilance lesson:
Leadership understood that **speed and pattern recognition** are everything in their industry. AI enhanced their ability to see weak signals of fraud early, instead of cleaning up damage after the fact.

Ask yourself: *Where do we face intelligent opponents—competitors, bad actors, or hostile forces—who adapt faster than our current systems can respond?*

Healthcare: Clinical Decision Support, Not Robot Doctors

Healthcare sits at the intersection of science, regulation, ethics, and human vulnerability. Mistakes cost lives.

In many hospitals and oncology centers, AI systems are increasingly used for **clinical decision support**, not as replacements for physicians. These tools:

- Scan medical literature far faster than any individual doctor
- Compare patient data with thousands of similar cases
- Suggest possible diagnoses, treatment options, or risk factors to consider

Human clinicians still make the final call. But AI helps:

- Surface options that might otherwise be missed

- Check for dangerous drug interactions or overlooked lab values
- Standardize care quality across providers and locations

Vigilance lesson:
Leadership in these organizations treats AI as a **second set of eyes, not a new boss**. They protect clinical judgment while using technology to reduce blind spots.

Ask yourself: *Where would a "second set of eyes" dramatically improve safety, consistency, or quality in my organization?*

4.3 The AI Foresight Playbook

You do not need a seven-figure budget to start using AI intelligently. You do need clarity, discipline, and the right questions.

Use this **AI Foresight Playbook** as a practical guide.

1. Start with Strategic Problems, Not Tools

Ask:

- What decisions are we making today with weak data or slow analysis?
- Where do delays, guesswork, or surprises hurt us most—financially, operationally, or reputationally?

Examples:

- Forecasting demand or staffing
- Detecting risk (fraud, safety incidents, quality issues)
- Prioritizing leads or customer outreach
- Monitoring critical assets or infrastructure

If a problem is vague, AI will give you vague value.

2. *Clarify the Data You Have—and the Data You Need*

Inventory your data:

- What do we actually collect today?
- Where is it stored? Who owns it? In what quality?
- Are there blind spots or silos that need to be broken down?

You don't need "perfect" data, but you do need **useful, reliable, and legally/ethically obtained** data.

3. *Choose Focused Use Cases*

Pick **one to three high-impact use cases** as pilots:

- Clear business value
- Clear owner
- Reasonable access to data

Examples:

- A churn model to identify at-risk customers
- A maintenance model to predict equipment failures
- A risk model to flag suspicious transactions

Resist the urge to "do AI everywhere." Earn credibility with one or two wins.

4. *Partner with the Right Expertise*

Depending on your size, that may mean:

- Internal data and IT teams
- Trusted vendors or platforms
- External consultants with domain and technical credibility

Your job as a leader is to demand:

- Clear problem definition
- Transparent assumptions
- Measurable outcomes

5. Pilot, Measure, and Refine

Run a limited pilot with:

- A controlled scope
- Baseline metrics (accuracy, speed, cost, revenue impact)
- A defined test period

Questions to review:

- Did AI improve accuracy or speed?
- Did it reduce risk or cost?
- Did it change behavior (how people make decisions) in the right way?

If not, **fix it, refocus it, or kill it.**

6. Put Guardrails Around Ethics, Security, and Bias

A vigilant leader cannot ignore:

- **Data privacy and security** – Who has access? How is data protected?
- **Bias and fairness** – Are models treating certain customers, employees, or groups unfairly?
- **Explainability** – Can we explain, at a reasonable level, how decisions are being made?

Set clear policies:

- What AI is allowed to influence
- What requires human review
- How you will audit and adjust models over time

7. Train Your People

AI without training creates fear and resistance.

- Explain **why** you're using AI and what it will and will not do.
- Train people on how to read dashboards, alerts, and recommendations.
- Emphasize that AI is a tool to **amplify their judgment**, not replace their value.

4.4 AI and the Five Pillars of Vigilant Leadership

AI is powerful only to the extent that it supports the way you lead. It should strengthen, not weaken, your Five Pillars.

- **Adaptability**
  AI helps you see change sooner—customer patterns, market moves, operational shifts—so you can adapt in weeks instead of years.
- **Proactive Problem-Solving**
  Predictive models turn **reactive firefighting** into **preventative maintenance**—whether in fraud, safety, or customer churn.
- **Resilience**
  Early warning systems, risk models, and simulations help you build buffers, contingencies, and backup plans before crises hit.
- **Ethical Decision-Making**
  AI magnifies both good and bad decisions. Vigilant leaders

insist on transparency, fairness, and responsible use, protecting people and reputation.
- **Continuous Learning**
  AI can power dashboards, experiments, and feedback loops that keep your organization learning from real data instead of relying on hunches and office politics.

AI does not change what good leadership is. It simply raises the stakes. Leaders who ignore it fall behind. Leaders who embrace it carelessly create new risks. Vigilant leaders do neither.

Chapter 4 Summary: AI as a Force Multiplier, Not a Shortcut

In this chapter, you:

- Framed AI as a **strategic tool for foresight and decision-making**, not a replacement for leadership.
- Saw how organizations in retail, finance, and healthcare use AI to predict demand, detect fraud, and support critical decisions.
- Built an **AI Foresight Playbook** to move from hype to targeted, results-based use cases.
- Connected AI to the **Five Pillars of Vigilant Leadership**, ensuring technology serves mission, ethics, and resilience—not the other way around.

The core message: **AI belongs in the hands of serious leaders who care about results, responsibility, and the long-term health of their organizations.**

Leader Actions This Week

Pick **two or three** and put them on your calendar:

- **Identify one high-impact AI use case.**
  Ask: "Where do we make important decisions with weak or slow data?" Write down one candidate problem.
- **Inventory your data.**
  With a trusted technical partner, sketch a one-page overview of what data you actually have and how reliable it is.
- **Meet with your risk or compliance leader.**
  Discuss what AI is already being used in your organization (formally or informally) and where the guardrails are weak or missing.
- **Start a small AI pilot.**
  Choose one focused pilot with a clear owner and measurable outcomes—no grand announcements, just disciplined testing.
- **Educate your leadership team.**
  Share a short briefing with your senior team: what AI you're exploring, why, and how it will support—not threaten—their roles.

Questions for Your Team

Use these questions in an executive meeting or strategy off-site:

1. **Where in our business would better prediction or faster pattern recognition create the most value or reduce the most risk?**
2. **What AI-related risks—data, ethics, security—concern you the most, and what are we doing about them now?**
3. **If we do nothing with AI over the next three years, what do we realistically risk losing—to competitors, to cost, or to changing customer expectations?**

When you finish this chapter, you should not be "awed" by AI. You should be clear-eyed:

- Where it fits
- Where it doesn't
- How to start using it as a vigilant, responsible, pro-growth leader

From here, we'll turn to **Agile and Scrum**, the operating systems that help you turn foresight—AI-powered or not—into fast, disciplined execution.

CHAPTER 5

AGILE AND SCRUM IN STRATEGIC PLANNING

Vigilant leaders don't just see change coming—they organize their teams to move faster than the disruption around them. That is where **Agile and Scrum** come in.

Agile and Scrum are not buzzwords reserved for software companies. They are practical ways to:

- Make decisions in shorter cycles
- Learn from real-world feedback instead of long, abstract plans
- Adjust quickly when conditions change

In other words, they are the **operating systems** of vigilant leadership.

This chapter will show you:

- What Agile really is (and isn't)
- How Scrum gives you a simple rhythm for turning strategy into action
- How leaders in different sectors use Agile to stay ahead
- How to adopt Agile practices without losing discipline or control

5.1 Agile Principles for Vigilant Leadership

What Agile Is

Agile began in the world of software but has grown into a broader **mindset and method** for handling complex, changing work. Instead of long, rigid plans that assume stability, Agile favors:

- Short planning cycles
- Frequent delivery of real value
- Constant feedback
- The ability to pivot when conditions change

For our purposes, think of Agile as:

A disciplined way of working in short cycles, learning quickly, and adjusting based on reality—not wishful thinking.

That is exactly what vigilant leaders need.

We'll focus on four core Agile principles and connect them directly to vigilant leadership:

1. Adaptability
2. Collaboration
3. Customer-Centricity
4. Iterative Planning and Continuous Feedback

---

1. Adaptability: Planning to Adjust

Traditional planning assumes the future will cooperate with your Gantt chart. Agile assumes it won't.

Instead of building one large, fixed plan and defending it at all costs, Agile leaders:

- Break work into smaller pieces
- Plan in shorter time horizons
- Expect that new information will arrive mid-stream

For a vigilant leader, adaptability means:

- Updating priorities when market, regulatory, or operational realities change
- Being willing to reallocate resources quickly
- Treating "change of plan" as responsible leadership, not failure

Adaptability directly reinforces the **Adaptability** and **Proactive Problem-Solving** pillars from Chapter 1. You still have a direction, but you are no longer chained to a plan that no longer fits.

---

2. Collaboration: Using the Full Brain of the Organization

Agile assumes that complex problems are solved best by **cross-functional teams**, not by one leader handing down the "right" answer.

Agile leaders:

- Bring people from different functions together (operations, tech, finance, customer-facing roles)
- Encourage open discussion of constraints, risks, and trade-offs
- Create environments where people can challenge ideas without challenging the mission

This kind of collaboration:

- Surfaces risks earlier (because different perspectives are in the room)

- Creates better solutions (because trade-offs are visible)
- Builds buy-in (because people helped shape the plan)

For vigilant leadership, collaboration is how you turn **weak signals from the front lines** into strong, coordinated action.

---

3. Customer-Centricity: Anchoring on Real Value

Agile was built on the idea that **value to the customer** matters more than internal preferences or legacy processes.

Agile leaders ask:

- What outcome does the customer actually care about?
- What is the smallest version of that value we can deliver quickly?
- What feedback do we need to prove we are on the right track?

Instead of launching massive initiatives after months of internal debate, Agile teams:

- Deliver smaller, usable improvements
- Measure customer response
- Decide what to enhance, cut, or rethink based on real results

For a vigilant leader, this is essential. If you are not anchored in **real customer value**, you can be fast and flexible—and still be irrelevant.

---

4. Iterative Planning and Continuous Feedback

Agile replaces big yearly planning events with **frequent, smaller planning cycles**.

The pattern looks like this:

1. Plan a short cycle of work (often 1–4 weeks)
2. Do the work
3. Review what was delivered and what was learned
4. Adjust priorities and plan the next cycle

This rhythm:

- Reduces the cost of mistakes (because cycles are shorter)
- Builds a culture of learning (every cycle includes reflection)
- Keeps strategy and execution connected (you adjust based on what actually happened)

For vigilant leaders, iterative planning and feedback link directly to **Continuous Learning** and **Resilience**. You're not waiting until year-end to discover a strategy failed—you're learning in real time.

5.2 Implementing Scrum for Strategic Execution

Agile is the philosophy. **Scrum** is one of the most widely used frameworks for putting that philosophy into practice.

You don't need to copy every detail from the software world. You do need to understand how Scrum structures work in a way that supports vigilance.

The Basics of Scrum

In its simplest form, Scrum has:

- **A small, cross-functional team**
- **Clear roles**
- **A prioritized list of work**
- **Short, time-boxed cycles called sprints**

Let's translate that into leadership language.

Roles (Simplified for Leaders)

- **Product Owner (PO)** – Responsible for **what** gets done and in what order. Represents the voice of the customer and the business.
- **Scrum Master (or Team Lead)** – Responsible for **how** the team works together. Removes obstacles, keeps the process running, protects focus.
- **Team Members** – The people who do the work—design, build, test, deliver, analyze.

In a non-technical organization, you might call these roles:

- **Vision Owner** (PO)
- **Process Owner** (Scrum Master)
- **Delivery Team**

The titles are less important than the clarity: someone owns **priority**, someone owns **process**, and the team owns **delivery**.

The Sprint Rhythm

A **sprint** is a fixed period—usually 1–4 weeks—during which the team commits to completing a specific set of work.

The basic sprint cycle includes:

1. **Sprint Planning** – The team decides what work they can realistically complete in the upcoming sprint, pulled from a prioritized backlog.

2. **Daily Stand-ups** – Short (10–15 minute) check-ins where the team aligns: What did we do? What will we do next? What's blocking us?
3. **Sprint Review** – At the end of the sprint, the team shows what was actually completed to stakeholders and gathers feedback.
4. **Sprint Retrospective** – The team reflects: What went well? What didn't? What will we change next time?

This rhythm is powerful for vigilant leaders because it:

- Forces regular, honest conversations about progress and obstacles
- Creates natural points to incorporate new information or adjust priorities
- Makes it hard to hide stagnation or drift—every sprint ends with a visible result

---

A Simple Scrum-Style Pilot (for Any Organization)

You don't have to transform your entire company to use Scrum. Try this with one important initiative:

1. **Choose a strategic project**
    - Example: improving customer onboarding, reducing a key operational delay, launching a new service.
2. **Form a small cross-functional team**
    - Include representatives from the functions that must cooperate for this to succeed.
3. **Create a basic backlog**
    - List the tasks and outcomes needed. Prioritize by impact and dependency.
4. **Set sprint length**
    - Start with 2-week sprints.

5. **Run at least 3 sprints**
   - Commit to the full cycle: plan → daily stand-ups → review → retrospective.
   - Adjust as you go, but don't abandon the structure after the first friction.
6. **Measure results**
   - Did you deliver more, faster, and with fewer surprises than your usual approach?
   - What did you learn that you can carry into other projects?

This pilot will tell you more about Agile's real-world fit in your organization than any book or seminar.

5.3 Case Studies: Agile in Action

Spotify – Structuring for Speed and Autonomy

Spotify popularized the language of **squads, tribes, chapters, and guilds**—cross-functional teams with a high degree of autonomy.

Key Agile moves:

- **Squads** owned specific parts of the user experience and could ship improvements without waiting for endless approvals.
- Leadership focused on **alignment and principles**, not micromanaging tasks.
- Frequent releases and real-time data allowed constant experimentation.

Vigilance lesson:
Spotify's structure allowed it to respond quickly to user behavior and competitive moves. The company was wired for continuous learning and adaptation, not rigid adherence to one plan.

Amazon – Relentless Iteration at Scale

We've already looked at Amazon as a master of logistics and foresight. They also apply Agile principles relentlessly:

- Small, empowered **"two-pizza teams"** handle specific services or features.
- New ideas are tested quickly—often starting as simple prototypes or limited tests.
- Data from real customer interactions drives what gets scaled and what gets killed.

Vigilance lesson:
Amazon doesn't just "plan big" and hope. It experiments, measures, and iterates constantly. Agile is how it keeps moving fast without completely losing control.

Salesforce – Continuous Delivery of Customer Value

Salesforce, a major cloud-based CRM provider, lives and dies on its ability to keep improving the platform without breaking customers' businesses.

Agile practices at Salesforce include:

- Regular release cycles with clear communication of changes
- Agile teams aligned around specific customer-facing capabilities
- Strong feedback loops between customers, support, and development

Vigilance lesson:
Salesforce uses Agile to stay aligned with evolving customer needs and the broader tech landscape. Their rhythm of regular, incremental

improvement keeps them relevant and reduces the risk of disruptive, painful "big bang" changes.

5.4 Benefits and Challenges of Agile Adoption

Benefits

When implemented with discipline, Agile and Scrum can:

- **Increase Speed and Flexibility**
  Short cycles and prioritized backlogs allow faster adjustment to new information.
- **Improve Transparency**
  Regular reviews and retrospectives make work, blockers, and results visible.
- **Boost Engagement**
  Teams that have a say in planning and problem-solving tend to be more motivated and invested.
- **Enhance Customer Alignment**
  Frequent feedback keeps you closer to what customers actually value now.

All of this directly supports **vigilant leadership**: you're listening, adjusting, and acting with greater precision and speed.

Challenges

Agile is not a magic switch. Leaders must be honest about the friction it creates:

- **Cultural Resistance**
  People used to rigid hierarchies may resist shared ownership, faster decision cycles, or transparent progress tracking.

- **Leadership Style Shift**
  Command-and-control leaders can struggle with Agile. The role shifts from "chief problem-solver" to "remover of obstacles and shaper of priorities."
- **Role Confusion**
  Without clear definition of roles (who sets priorities, who owns process, who delivers), Agile quickly turns into chaos.
- **Scaling Across the Organization**
  Agile is easier on one team than across dozens. Scaling requires intentional design and strong alignment on values and goals.

Vigilant leaders address these challenges directly. They:

- Communicate why Agile matters
- Model the behaviors they expect
- Start small, learn, and expand thoughtfully instead of forcing a rushed, organization-wide mandate

Chapter 5 Summary: Agile as the Operating System of Vigilant Leadership

In this chapter, you:

- Framed Agile as a **disciplined way of working in short cycles**, learning quickly, and adapting based on reality.
- Saw how **Scrum** provides a practical rhythm—sprints, planning, reviews, retrospectives—for turning strategy into action.
- Looked at real-world examples (Spotify, Amazon, Salesforce) of Agile in different industries.
- Weighed the **benefits** (speed, transparency, engagement, customer alignment) against the **challenges** (culture, leadership style, role clarity, scaling).

The key idea: **Agile and Scrum give vigilant leaders the structure they need to move fast without losing control.**

Leader Actions This Week

Choose at least **two** and schedule them:

- **Identify one project for an Agile pilot.**
  Pick a strategic initiative and commit to running it in 2–4 week sprints for the next 60–90 days.
- **Form a cross-functional team.**
  Assemble a small group representing the key functions needed for that project. Clarify who owns priorities and who owns process.
- **Run a simple sprint planning meeting.**
  Define the goal of the next sprint and agree on the small set of tasks the team can realistically deliver.
- **Hold daily stand-ups for two weeks.**
  Keep them short. Ask: "What did you do? What will you do next? What's blocking you?"
- **Run your first retrospective.**
  At the end of the sprint, take 30 minutes to ask: "What worked, what didn't, and what will we change next time?"

Questions for Your Team

Use these in a leadership meeting or workshop:

1. **Where do long, rigid plans hurt us the most when reality shifts?**
2. **If we adopted 2-week sprints for one strategic project, what might improve—and what are we afraid of?**

3. **What leadership behaviors (including mine) would need to change for Agile to work here?**

With Agile and Scrum in place, the tools from earlier chapters—PEST, SWOT, scenarios, AI, and industry foresight—become far more powerful. You won't just see threats and opportunities; you'll have the **muscle** to respond quickly and intelligently.

Next, we'll turn to **weak signals**—the subtle early warnings most leaders miss—and how vigilant leaders learn to detect and interpret them before everyone else.

CHAPTER 6

MASTERING WEAK SIGNAL INTERPRETATION

Most leaders react to what everyone else can already see.

Vigilant leaders train themselves—and their organizations—to notice what others ignore: **weak signals**. These are small, early indicators of bigger changes to come: a shift in customer behavior, a pattern in complaints, a new competitor no one is taking seriously, a subtle change in regulations, an uptick in minor incidents.

By the time a threat is obvious, your options are limited and expensive. When it's still a weak signal, you usually have **time, flexibility, and leverage**.

This chapter will help you:

- Understand what weak signals are and why they matter
- Build habits and systems that surface them early
- Separate noise from signal
- Turn early hints into thoughtful decisions and practical action

---

6.1 What Are Weak Signals?

A **weak signal** is:

A small, early sign that something important may be changing—before it shows up in headline metrics or obvious crises.

Examples:

- A specific type of customer complaint quietly increases over a few months
- A competitor starts offering an unusual pricing model in one region
- A junior employee points out a recurring glitch no one has "had time" to address
- A regulator makes a comment that hints at future rule changes
- A new technology is adopted first by hobbyists and niche players, not big incumbents

Individually, any one of these may seem trivial. Together, they can reveal:

- Shifts in customer expectations
- Emerging risks in safety, quality, or security
- New forms of competition
- Political or regulatory changes that will reshape your environment

Weak signals rarely arrive in a neat report. They show up as fragments of information scattered across your organization and environment. Vigilant leadership is the discipline of **noticing, probing, and acting** on those fragments before they become emergencies.

6.2 Sensing Weak Signals: Building Your Early Warning System

Weak signals are everywhere. The question is whether you have the **eyes, ears, and channels** to notice them.

Sources of Weak Signals

Common sources include:

- **Front-line employees**
  They see problems, workarounds, and customer reactions in real time.
- **Customers and clients**
  Complaints, suggestions, and odd requests often point to emerging needs or frustrations.
- **Operational data**
  Near misses, minor defects, delays, maintenance calls, safety observations.
- **Vendors and partners**
  They see trends across multiple clients and often know what's changing earlier than you do.
- **Industry news and niche players**
  Small companies and early adopters experiment in ways big incumbents often ignore.
- **Regulators and policymakers**
  Hearings, speeches, draft proposals, and enforcement patterns hint at where rules are heading.

Vigilant leaders **design** ways to listen to these sources, not just hope information will "bubble up."

Habits of a Weak-Signal-Sensitive Leader

You can dramatically increase what you catch by changing a few habits:

- **Ask different questions.**
  Instead of only "How are the numbers?" ask:
    - "What's bothering you that we're not talking about?"
    - "What are customers starting to ask for that we don't offer?"

- o "Where do you see small problems repeating?"
- **Create safe reporting channels.**
  Encourage people to raise concerns without fear of punishment or ridicule. That might include anonymous feedback, regular skip-level meetings, or disciplined after-action reviews.
- **Walk the floor.**
  Spend time where the work happens—sites, shops, plants, call centers, front desks. Look for patterns: repeated workarounds, frustrated expressions, tools people don't use, corners that get cut.
- **Scan beyond your bubble.**
  Read outside your exact niche. Watch how adjacent industries respond to technology, regulation, or social shifts. Many "surprises" in one field were visible earlier in another.
- **Use your tools.**
  AI dashboards, customer analytics, safety/incident reporting systems—these can all surface subtle trends if you configure them to look for small drifts, not just big spikes.

The point is not paranoia. It is **disciplined curiosity**.

6.3 Probing and Making Sense of Weak Signals

Not every odd data point or complaint deserves a strategic reaction. Vigilant leaders learn to **probe** weak signals before overreacting or ignoring them.

Step 1: Collect and Cluster

When you notice a potential weak signal:

- Write it down.
- Look for **similar signals** from other sources:
    - Are multiple customers hinting at the same issue?
    - Are different teams seeing related problems?
    - Has this come up before in a different form?

Sometimes what looks like "one-off noise" is actually part of a broader pattern.

Step 2: Ask "Why?"—More Than Once

Simple tools, used seriously, are powerful.

- **Five Whys**
  Start with the symptom and ask "Why?" repeatedly until you reach a root cause or deeper pattern.
  Example:
    - We're seeing more last-minute order changes. Why?
    - Because customers say they weren't sure about their needs. Why?
    - Because our options are confusing and we don't guide them well. Why?
    - Because we removed human support to cut costs.

  Suddenly, the "weak signal" of order changes points to a deeper issue: we may be saving money in the short term while eroding trust and clarity.

Step 3: Cross-Functional Conversation

Weak signals often cross boundaries. Bring in people from different areas:

- Operations
- Sales / customer service
- Finance

- Technology / data
- Legal / risk (if relevant)

Ask together:

- "What might this mean?"
- "Where else could this be happening?"
- "If this grew 10x, what would break?"

Cross-functional perspectives help prevent narrow interpretations and reveal systemic issues.

Step 4: Consider the Context

Not every weak signal is equally important. Use what you built in Chapters 2 and 3:

- **PEST:** Does this signal relate to a political, economic, social, or technological trend you already identified?
- **SWOT:** Does it expose a weakness or threaten a strength?
- **Scenarios:** Is this signal consistent with one of the futures you considered?

If a weak signal aligns with an existing risk or scenario, it deserves more attention than an isolated oddity.

6.4 From Signals to Decisions

The hardest part is knowing **when to act**. Move too early and you waste resources. Move too late and you pay a much higher price.

Vigilant leaders use three lenses:

1. Impact vs. Likelihood

Ask:

- If this signal represents a real trend, **how big could the impact be** (on safety, finances, reputation, mission)?
- How **likely** is it that this trend is real, not random noise?

High-impact, high-likelihood signals demand action now.
High-impact, low-certainty signals demand **monitoring and low-cost experiments**.
Low-impact signals may simply be logged and watched.

2. Reversibility

Some actions are hard to reverse; others are cheap to roll back.

Examples:

- Training your staff on a new safety procedure: low risk, highly reversible.
- Selling a major business unit: high risk, not easily reversible.

With weak signals, look for **reversible moves** first:

- Small process changes
- Pilot projects
- A/B tests
- Updated messaging
- Targeted investments in data or monitoring

You can learn a lot from small moves without betting the company.

3. Decision Loops, Not One-Off Choices

Treat weak-signal decisions as **loops**, not single events:

1. See something
2. Run a small test or make a small adjustment
3. Measure the result
4. Decide whether to expand, adjust, or stop

This is where Agile and Scrum (Chapter 5) support vigilance. Short sprints and regular retrospectives are ideal for testing weak-signal-driven ideas without derailing the entire organization.

6.5 The Weak Signal Toolkit

To make this practical, here is a concise toolkit you can adapt to your organization.

1. Weak Signal Log

Create a simple, shared log (spreadsheet, form, or system) where leaders and key staff can record:

- Date
- Source (customer, employee, partner, data, news, etc.)
- Description of the signal
- Initial thoughts on potential impact

Review this log regularly in leadership or foresight meetings.

2. Monthly "Signals and Surprises" Meeting

Once a month, add a standing agenda item:

- "What weak signals are we seeing?"
- "What surprised us this month?"
- "What did we learn that challenges our assumptions?"

Tie these directly to your **PEST, SWOT, and scenarios** so signals feed your broader strategic view.

3. Early Warning Indicators

For your top threats and critical assumptions, define **leading indicators**:

- What would we see **first** if this risk were becoming real?
- What specific metrics, behaviors, or events should we track?

Assign owners to monitor each indicator and report changes.

4. Small Experiment Protocol

When a weak signal looks promising or worrying, use a simple protocol:

- Define the question: "What are we trying to learn?"
- Design a small-scale test: "What is the smallest experiment that would give us useful data?"
- Set a clear timeframe and metrics.
- Run the test.
- Decide: expand, modify, or stop.

This prevents endless discussion and pushes the organization toward **learning by doing**.

5. Cultural Reinforcement

Weak signal work dies fast in cultures where:

- People are punished for raising inconvenient truths
- Leaders are defensive when challenged
- Teams are too busy firefighting to think

Reinforce vigilance by:

- Publicly thanking those who surface meaningful weak signals
- Incorporating signal discussion into regular meetings
- Modeling humility: "I hadn't seen that—thank you."

Chapter 6 Summary: Seeing What Others Miss

In this chapter, you:

- Defined **weak signals** as early hints of important change
- Identified key sources—front line, customers, ops data, partners, regulators, and niche players
- Learned how to **sense, cluster, and probe** weak signals instead of dismissing them or overreacting
- Used **impact, likelihood, and reversibility** to decide when and how to act
- Built a **Weak Signal Toolkit** to embed this work into your regular leadership rhythm

The core message: **vigilant leaders don't wait for clarity that never comes. They act on well-judged early warnings while they still have time to shape events, instead of merely surviving them.**

Leader Actions This Week

Choose at least **two**:

- **Start a weak signal log.**
  Create a simple shared document and ask your direct reports to add anything they believe "might be nothing—but might be something" over the next month.

- **Add one question to your check-ins.**
  In one-on-ones and team meetings, ask: "What small problems or patterns are you seeing that worry you?"
- **Review recent surprises.**
  Look back over the last 6–12 months. Identify three negative surprises and ask: "What weak signals did we miss?"
- **Design one small experiment.**
  Pick a weak signal tied to customers, operations, or risk. Run a low-cost, time-limited test to learn more.
- **Assign indicator owners.**
  For your top two strategic threats, define 2–3 early-warning indicators and assign a person to monitor each.

Questions for Your Team

Use these in a strategy or leadership session:

1. **Where in our organization are weak signals most likely to appear first—and are we really listening there?**
2. **What keeps people from raising early concerns or unconventional ideas?**
3. **If we had paid serious attention to a weak signal in the past, which painful problem might we have avoided—or turned into an opportunity?**

Mastering weak signals does not mean you will predict everything. It does mean you will be less surprised, more prepared, and far better positioned than leaders who only react when a crisis finally crashes through the front door.

Next, we'll turn to **resilience**—how to build organizations that can absorb shocks, adapt, and come back stronger when the unexpected arrives.

CHAPTER 7

BUILDING RESILIENCE

Foresight is valuable only if your organization can take a hit and keep moving.

Resilience is the capacity to **absorb shocks, adapt under pressure, and come back stronger** instead of collapsing or drifting. It is not about pretending everything is fine or hoping crises never arrive. It is about building the strength, structure, and culture to handle them when they do.

In this chapter, we will focus on:

- Turning foresight into concrete resilience plans
- Using simulations and stress tests to expose weak points before reality does
- Building a culture of continuous improvement and learning
- Strengthening your business model, supply chains, and strategic alliances for uncertain times

7.1 Turning Foresight into Resilient Plans

Chapters 2, 3, and 6 helped you **see** what might be coming: PEST, SWOT, scenarios, industry foresight, and weak signals. Now we convert that insight into **practical resilience**.

Resilience planning answers three questions:

1. What could realistically hit us?
2. How would it hurt us?
3. What can we put in place now so we are bruised, not broken?

Dynamic Risk Assessment

Begin with a clear-eyed view of your major risks:

- Financial (cash flow, credit, interest rates, key customers)
- Operational (facilities, equipment, systems, data)
- People (critical roles, leadership continuity, safety)
- Legal and regulatory (compliance, liability, reputational exposure)
- Strategic (disruption, new entrants, technological shifts)

For each top risk:

- Estimate **impact** (if this happens, how bad is it?)
- Estimate **likelihood** (how realistic is it in the next 1–3 years?)
- Identify **current controls** (what are we already doing?)
- Decide **what additional protection** is needed (processes, policies, reserves, diversification)

This is not about creating a 200-page risk manual. It is about making sure you are not blindsided by obvious vulnerabilities.

Redundancy and Margin

Resilient organizations build **margin**:

- Financial margin – conservative debt levels, cash reserves, access to credit
- Operational margin – backup suppliers, spare capacity, alternative routes or locations
- People margin – cross-trained staff, succession plans, bench strength

Margin costs something in the short term. It is also what keeps you in the game when others are forced into desperate moves.

Ask:

- Where are we running so lean that a single disruption would stop us?
- Where could targeted redundancy—one extra supplier, one backup system, one cross-trained role—dramatically reduce our exposure?

Simulations and Wargaming

You do not want the first time your team faces a serious disruption to be the real thing.

Simulations and wargames:

- Create realistic scenarios: cyberattack, loss of a major customer, plant shutdown, regulatory hit, key leader exit
- Ask your leadership team: "If this happened tomorrow, what would we do in the first 24–72 hours?"
- Walk through communication, decision-making, and operational steps
- Identify confusion, bottlenecks, and gaps in responsibility

Resilient leaders do not use simulations to scare people; they use them to **clarify roles, expose flaws, and strengthen confidence**.

A simple rule: if a scenario would severely damage you and you have never walked through it with your team, you are not as resilient as you think.

7.2 Culture of Continuous Improvement

Systems and plans matter. Culture is what keeps resilience alive when no one is watching.

A **continuous improvement culture** is one where:

- People are encouraged to identify problems and suggest fixes
- Small improvements are celebrated, not dismissed as trivial
- Mistakes are analyzed for learning, not just punished
- Processes, not just individuals, are examined when something goes wrong

This culture directly supports resilience. It turns every small issue into an opportunity to strengthen the organization.

Practical Levers for Continuous Improvement

You don't need a complex methodology to start. Focus on a few simple practices:

- **After-Action Reviews (AARs)**
  After major projects, incidents, or crises, ask:
    - What did we intend to happen?
    - What actually happened?
    - What went well and why?
    - What went poorly and why?
    - What will we do differently next time?

  Keep these conversations honest but constructive.

- **Suggestion and Fix-It Channels**
  Create a simple way for employees to suggest improvements and report recurring problems.

- o Respond visibly—either implement the idea or explain why not.
- o Track and share small wins regularly.
- **Standard Work and Refinement**
  Document key processes so they are not dependent on memory or heroics.
    - o Once documented, invite front-line staff to propose changes that improve safety, speed, or quality.
- **Learning Rhythm**
  Encourage and support ongoing learning:
    - o Short internal workshops
    - o Peer-to-peer teaching
    - o Targeted external courses or certifications tied directly to your mission

Tools and platforms can help, but the central message must be clear: **we are a learning organization, not a static one.**

7.3 Strategies for Navigating Uncertainty

Uncertainty is not going away. Resilient organizations do not just endure it; they use it to sharpen their edge.

Here are four strategic lenses to apply.

1. Stress-Test Your Business Model

Using your scenarios from Chapter 2 and your industry foresight from Chapter 3, ask:

- If revenue dropped by 20–30% for 6–12 months, what would fail first?
- If a key cost (energy, materials, labor) spiked, how would that affect our margins?

- If one or two major customers left, how exposed would we be?
- What if a new competitor offered a similar product at a lower price or with a different model?

Identify:

- **Fixed costs** that could be made more variable
- **Concentration risks** (too much dependence on one customer, supplier, or region)
- **Pricing and value levers** you could pull under pressure (bundling, service tiers, premium offerings)

Your goal is not to eliminate all risk. It is to avoid a business model so fragile that modest shocks become existential.

2. Strengthen Supply Chain and Vendor Resilience

Recent years have exposed how vulnerable supply chains can be.

Resilient leaders:

- Map critical suppliers and logistics routes
- Identify single points of failure—especially for key inputs, technology systems, or specialized services
- Develop **backup options**: alternative suppliers, multiple shipping methods, inventory buffers where appropriate
- Build strong relationships with strategic partners, so you are not just a name on a spreadsheet when prioritization decisions must be made

Ask: *If our most critical supplier failed tomorrow, what would we do?*

3. Look for Opportunity in Disruption

Resilience is not only defensive. Leaders with a vigilant mindset understand that downturns and disruptions can be **entry points**:

- Competitors may be distracted, overleveraged, or unable to invest
- Customers may be open to new solutions as their old ones fail
- Assets (talent, facilities, acquisitions) may become available at better value

Questions to consider:

- If our industry faces a downturn, where might we **gain market share** while others retreat?
- What capabilities could we build now that position us to move quickly when conditions improve?
- Are there partnerships, acquisitions, or new offerings that only become realistic in a disrupted environment?

Resilience is the platform that allows you to go on offense when others are forced into defense.

4. Build Strategic Alliances

No organization is resilient in isolation. Strategic alliances and partnerships can:

- Expand your access to markets, technology, talent, or capacity
- Share risk on large initiatives
- Provide mutual support in crises (backup facilities, shared logistics, co-marketing)

Be deliberate:

- Identify partners whose strengths complement your weaknesses
- Define clear expectations, boundaries, and exit options
- Keep alliances aligned with your values and long-term strategy

Resilient leaders invest time in **relationships before they are desperately needed**.

Chapter 7 Summary: Strength Built Before the Storm

In this chapter, you:

- Turned foresight into **resilience planning**—dynamic risk assessment, redundancy, and simulations
- Saw how a **culture of continuous improvement** turns small issues into chances to strengthen your systems
- Learned to **stress-test your business model**, shore up supply chains, and think offensively about opportunity in disruption
- Recognized the importance of **strategic alliances** as part of your resilience strategy

The core message: **resilience is built long before the crisis.** It is the result of disciplined decisions, margin, and culture—not luck.

Leader Actions This Week

Choose at least **two**:

- **Name your top five risks.**
  With your leadership team, list the five most serious risks your organization faces in the next 1–3 years. For each, identify one mitigation step you can start this quarter.

- **Identify one fragile point.**
  Ask: "Where are we one failure away from major disruption?" (supplier, system, person, site). Develop at least a basic backup plan.
- **Schedule a simple wargame.**
  Pick one scenario (loss of a major customer, system outage, regulatory shock) and spend 60–90 minutes walking through your response. Capture gaps and assign follow-up actions.
- **Launch or strengthen after-action reviews.**
  For the next significant project or incident, run a short AAR and document 2–3 concrete changes you will make.
- **Review your financial margin.**
  With your finance lead, assess your cash position, debt, and access to credit. Ask what would need to change for you to withstand a 20–30% revenue shock for 6–12 months.

Questions for Your Team

Use these in a leadership or board-level discussion:

1. **If we faced a major disruption tomorrow, what would we regret not having put in place today?**
2. **Where are we depending too heavily on "heroic effort" instead of solid systems and backups?**
3. **In the last crisis we faced, what did we handle well—and what did we only survive by luck or overwork? What are we doing to fix that now?**

Resilience does not make you immune to adversity; it makes you **effective in adversity**. Combined with the vigilance you've developed in earlier chapters, it gives you the strength to protect your people, honor your commitments, and capitalize on opportunities that less prepared leaders never see.

Next, we will turn to **crisis management**—the moment when all your preparation is tested—and build a clear playbook for leading under maximum pressure.

CHAPTER 8

CRISIS MANAGEMENT: LEADING WHEN IT MATTERS MOST

Everything you've built as a vigilant leader—foresight, resilience, culture, and systems—gets tested in crisis.

A **crisis** is not just a bad day. It is a moment when:

- Safety, reputation, or the survival of the organization are at stake
- Events are moving faster than normal decision cycles
- People are anxious, angry, or afraid
- Information is incomplete, conflicting, or changing by the hour

In these moments, leadership is not theoretical. It is visible, immediate, and consequential.

This chapter will give you:

- A clear distinction between routine problems and true crises
- A practical framework for **before, during, and after** a crisis
- Guidance on communication, decision-making, and emotional control under pressure
- A simple crisis playbook you can adapt for your organization

8.1 Crisis vs. Routine Problems

Not every tough situation is a crisis. If everything is a crisis, then nothing is.

A situation becomes a **crisis** when it:

- Poses a serious threat to life, health, trust, or survival
- Requires fast, coordinated decisions under pressure
- Draws intense attention from employees, customers, media, regulators, or the public
- Overwhelms normal procedures and escalation paths

Examples:

- Major safety incident or workplace fatality
- Large-scale data breach or cyberattack
- Public scandal involving ethics, fraud, or harassment
- Natural disaster, facility shutdown, or significant infrastructure failure
- Sudden loss of a key leader or major customer

Routine problems can be handled through normal processes. Crises require:

- **Clear authority**
- **Rapid but grounded decisions**
- **Deliberate communication**
- **Visible leadership presence**

Vigilant leaders resist the urge to label everything a crisis, but when a real crisis hits, they respond without hesitation.

8.2 Before the Crisis: Preparation and Structure

The worst time to design a crisis response is **in the middle of one**. Most of crisis management is built **before** the alarm ever sounds.

1. Define What a Crisis Is—For You

Clarify, in writing:

- What types of events automatically trigger your crisis protocols
- Who has the authority to declare a crisis
- What thresholds (financial loss, safety impact, public attention, legal exposure) move a situation from "serious issue" to "crisis"

This reduces hesitation and argument when speed matters.

2. Establish a Crisis Team

Identify a small, cross-functional **Crisis Management Team (CMT)**:

- Senior leader (overall incident commander)
- Operations lead
- HR/People lead
- Legal/risk/compliance lead
- Communications/PR lead
- Technology/IT lead (if applicable)

Document:

- Primary and backup members
- How they are contacted (day, night, weekend)
- Where they will meet (physical or virtual war room)

3. Clarify Roles and Decision Rights

In a crisis, confusion about authority costs time and creates conflicting messages.

Decide in advance:

- Who **owns final decisions** in different types of crises (safety, cyber, financial, reputational)
- Who speaks internally
- Who speaks externally
- Who manages liaison with regulators, law enforcement, or external partners

Write this down. Make sure your leadership bench understands it.

4. Prepare Core Protocols and Checklists

You do not need a thick manual, but you do need:

- A basic **notification and escalation protocol**
- A **contact list** for key stakeholders (boards, regulators, major customers, media contacts, insurers)
- Templates for initial internal and external statements
- A simple framework for documenting what happens in real time

These tools reduce cognitive load when stress is high.

5. Train and Drill

At least once a year:

- Run a tabletop exercise (wargame) for one or two plausible crisis scenarios

- Walk through who would do what, who would say what, and what decisions would be needed
- Capture gaps and refine your plan

Preparedness is not paranoia. It is respect for reality.

8.3 During the Crisis: The Leader's Playbook

When crisis hits, the vigilant leader's job can be summarized in three words:

Stabilize. Communicate. Decide.

Everything else supports those three tasks.

Step 1: Stabilize the Situation

Your first priority is **life and safety**. Always.

Ask immediately:

- Is anyone in danger right now?
- What must we do in the next minutes and hours to protect life and safety?
- What must be shut down, secured, or isolated to prevent further harm?

Only after safety is addressed do you move to stabilizing operations and information:

- Stop the bleeding—contain damage where possible
- Confirm what systems or locations are affected
- Activate the pre-defined crisis team and protocols

Step 2: Get Ground Truth (As Best You Can)

You will not have perfect information. You must still act.

Focus on:

- Verifiable facts: What do we know for certain?
- Known unknowns: What do we know we don't know yet?
- Sources: Who is closest to the situation with the most reliable insight?

Avoid:

- Speculation masquerading as fact
- Overconfidence based on incomplete data
- Paralysis while you wait for 100% clarity

Vigilant leaders make the best decision they can with the information available, then adjust as new facts emerge.

Step 3: Communicate Clearly and Consistently

In a crisis, **silence is rarely neutral**. It creates anxiety and a vacuum that rumors will fill.

Your communication must be:

- **Timely** – Communicate early, even if you don't have all the answers.
- **Honest** – Share what you know and what you don't. Avoid spin.
- **Calm** – Tone matters. People take emotional cues from you.
- **Aligned** – Internal and external messages must match.

Consider three audiences:

1. **Internal (employees, key leaders)**
    - What happened (as far as you know).
    - What you are doing right now.
    - What you need from them.
    - When they will hear from you again.
2. **External (customers, partners, vendors)**
    - How it affects them.
    - What you are doing to address it.
    - Any immediate actions they should take.
    - How and when they can get updates.
3. **Regulators, authorities, and media (if applicable)**
    - Coordinate with legal and compliance.
    - Stay factual; do not speculate or assign blame prematurely.
    - Be respectful and responsive without surrendering control of your message.

A simple message framework:

- Here is what we know.
- Here is what we are doing.
- Here is how it affects you.
- Here is what we will do next and when you'll hear from us again.

Step 4: Lead Yourself – Emotional Intelligence Under Fire

Under crisis pressure, people watch the leader not just for instructions, but for **emotional signals**.

Key emotional intelligence disciplines:

- **Self-awareness** – Notice your own stress reactions. Are you becoming sharp, withdrawn, scattered?

- **Self-regulation** – Control your tone, body language, and pace. Breathe. Speak more slowly than you feel.
- **Empathy** – Acknowledge fear, loss, or frustration. You don't have to be sentimental, but you must be human.
- **Composure** – You cannot promise outcomes you don't control, but you can project steadiness and commitment.

Simple practices:

- Take brief pauses between intense conversations.
- Use a trusted advisor to check your tone and messaging.
- Avoid venting down; if you must vent, do it peer-to-peer, not to your team.

Your presence in crisis either **amplifies panic** or **anchors stability**. There is no neutral.

Step 5: Make Decisions Under Pressure

In crisis, no decision is also a decision—and usually a bad one.

Use a simple framework:

1. **Clarify the objective.**
    - What are we trying to protect or achieve first? (life, safety, containment, trust, continuity)
2. **List real options.**
    - What can we actually do in the next hours and days? Not in theory—practically.
3. **Weigh trade-offs.**
    - For each option, what are the risks, costs, and likely outcomes?
    - What aligns best with our values and long-term mission?
4. **Decide and assign.**

o   Choose. Name who is responsible for execution. Set time frames.
5. **Review and adjust.**
   o   As new facts appear, be willing to refine your decision, but not to waffle endlessly.

Remember:

- In a true crisis, **speed and clarity** often matter more than perfection.
- Ethical shortcuts may look tempting; they almost always cost more later.
- A "good, timely decision" that you can defend is better than a "perfect" decision that never leaves the whiteboard.

Step 6: Manage Stakeholders Deliberately

Stakeholders in crisis include:

- Employees and their families
- Customers and clients
- Partners, vendors, and investors
- Regulators, community leaders, and, in some cases, the media

You cannot please everyone. You must:

- Prioritize safety and integrity
- Communicate respectfully and consistently
- Be willing to say "We don't know yet, but here is what we are doing to find out"

Stakeholder management is not about spin. It is about preserving **trust and working relationships** while you navigate a difficult reality.

Step 7: Use Technology Wisely

Technology can help—and it can distract.

Use it for:

- Rapid internal alerts and coordination (secure messaging, dashboards, status boards)
- Monitoring the situation (incident tracking, news, social media for emerging narratives)
- Documenting decisions and actions in real time

Avoid:

- Getting lost in feeds and noise
- Responding emotionally to every online comment
- Making statements on public platforms before your own people are informed

Technology should support your crisis plan, not drive it.

8.4 After the Crisis: Learn, Repair, Strengthen

When the immediate crisis is contained, many leaders are tempted to "move on" as quickly as possible. That is a mistake.

A crisis is costly. You owe it to your people and your mission to **extract maximum learning and long-term benefit**.

1. Conduct a Structured Debrief

Within days or weeks (depending on scale):

- Bring key leaders and front-line representatives together

- Create a timeline of what happened and when
- Ask:
  - What did we do well?
  - What did we do poorly or too slowly?
  - Where did our systems support us—and where did they fail?
  - Where did communication break down?

Document the findings. Avoid witch hunts. Focus on systems, processes, and decision points more than individual blame.

2. Address Harm and Repair Trust

If people were hurt—physically, emotionally, or financially—address it directly:

- Acknowledge what happened without evasive language
- Take responsibility where appropriate
- Offer reasonable remedies or support within your means
- Follow through on any commitments you make

Trust is earned or lost here. How you handle the **aftermath** often matters more than the original incident in the minds of your people and your customers.

3. Fix Root Causes

Tie back to your **weak signal and resilience work**:

- Which risks materialized that you had identified—but not addressed?
- Which new vulnerabilities did this crisis reveal?
- What policies, training, systems, or structures must change?

Assign owners and timelines. Track progress. Do not let the same weaknesses sit untouched until the next crisis.

4. Update Plans and Training

Based on what you learned:

- Update your crisis protocols, contact lists, and templates
- Refine your definition of "crisis" if needed
- Use this incident as a scenario in future drills so you do not repeat the experience the same way

This is how you convert pain into **institutional maturity**.

5. Reframe the Narrative

Internally and, where appropriate, externally:

- Tell the truth about what happened
- Highlight where people showed courage, integrity, and commitment
- Share what you are changing as a result

You are not rewriting history. You are helping your organization **make sense of the event** in a way that strengthens identity and resolve instead of leaving only scars and rumors.

Chapter 8 Summary: Crisis as the Ultimate Test of Vigilance

In this chapter, you:

- Distinguished true **crises** from routine problems
- Built a **before/during/after** framework for crisis management
- Defined concrete steps for preparation: crisis team, roles, protocols, and drills

- Learned how to lead **during** crisis: stabilize, get ground truth, communicate, manage yourself, decide, and coordinate stakeholders
- Saw how to handle the **aftermath**: debrief, repair trust, fix root causes, update plans, and reframe the narrative

The core message: **crisis is not the time to invent your leadership. It is the time to reveal it.** Vigilant leaders prepare in advance, lead with clarity and integrity in the moment, and emerge from crisis wiser and stronger.

Leader Actions This Month

Crisis work requires more than a week. Over the next 30–60 days, choose at least **three**:

- **Define your crisis triggers.**
  With your leadership team, agree on what qualifies as a crisis in your context and who has authority to declare one.
- **Form or confirm a crisis team.**
  Name core members and backups from key functions. Build and share a contact sheet.
- **Create or update a basic crisis playbook.**
  Include: activation criteria, roles, communication templates, and key stakeholder contact lists.
- **Run one tabletop exercise.**
  Choose a plausible crisis scenario and walk leadership through the first 24–72 hours. Capture gaps and assign follow-ups.
- **Review communication protocols.**
  Ensure you can reach your people quickly and clearly, even if primary systems fail (alternate channels, backups).

- **Identify one past "near miss" or crisis.**
  Conduct a brief after-action review and implement at least one structural improvement.

Questions for Your Team

Use these for a board discussion, off-site, or senior leadership meeting:

1. **If a serious crisis hit us tomorrow, who would be in charge—and does everyone know that?**
2. **In our last major incident, did we communicate too little, too late, or too cautiously? What would we do differently now?**
3. **What are we most afraid of discovering if we ran a real crisis drill? And what does that tell us about our current readiness?**

Crisis management is not a separate discipline from vigilant leadership; it is **where vigilant leadership shows its true value**. If you have done the work of foresight, resilience, and culture-building, you will not be invincible—but you will be far more effective, honorable, and steady when the pressure is highest.

Afterword: Thank You and a Final Charge

Thank you for investing your time and attention in this book.

You did not pick up a leadership book to be entertained. You picked it up because you carry real responsibility—for people, for customers, for capital, and for the future of your organization. That alone already separates you from the crowd.

You now have:

- A clear definition of **vigilant leadership**
- A framework in the **Five Pillars**
- Tools for **threat identification, foresight, weak signals, AI, Agile, resilience, and crisis management**

The question is no longer whether you understand these ideas. The question is: **What will you do with them?**

Vigilance is not a personality trait. It is a daily decision. Every day you either drift toward comfort and distraction, or you move toward clarity, discipline, and courage.

My charge to you is simple:

- Choose vigilance.
- Build margin.
- Tell the truth.
- Protect your people.
- Act before you are forced.

If you do, you will not only strengthen your organization—you will become the kind of leader others are proud to follow.

Are You Ready?

A 90-Day Vigilant Leader Plan

Use this as a simple, practical roadmap. You do not need to do everything perfectly. You do need to start.

Days 1–30: Clarify and See

- Re-read your notes from Chapters 1–3.
- Write a one-sentence definition of **vigilant leadership** in your own words.
- Run a short **PEST scan** with your team.
- Build a one-page **SWOT** that reflects your real position.
- Identify your **top three external forces** and **top three internal vulnerabilities**.

Output by Day 30:
A concise, honest picture of where you stand and what is pressing on you.

Days 31–60: Build Muscle

- Choose **one AI or analytics use case** to explore, even in simple form.
- Launch a **Scrum-style pilot** on one strategic project (2–4 week sprints).
- Start a **weak signal log** and add "What are you seeing that worries you?" to your regular meetings.
- Name your **top five risks** and agree on at least one mitigation step for each.

Output by Day 60:
Evidence that you are not only seeing more—you are acting differently.

Days 61–90: Lock In Resilience

- Identify at least **one single point of failure** and start a concrete backup plan.
- Run at least **one tabletop crisis exercise** with your leadership team.
- Conduct an **after-action review** on a recent project or incident and implement 2–3 process improvements.
- Draft or update a **basic crisis playbook** (roles, triggers, contact lists, communication templates).

Output by Day 90:
A stronger, more honest, more prepared organization—with you at the center, leading it deliberately instead of reacting by habit.

At the end of these 90 days, you will not be "done." But you will be a different leader than when you started—and people will feel the difference.

Appendix A: Recommended Resources

Use this list as a starting point for deeper study. You do not need them all; choose what fits your context and goals.

Books on Leadership and Organizational Health

- *Good to Great* – Jim Collins
- *Built to Last* – Jim Collins and Jerry Porras
- *The Advantage* – Patrick Lencioni
- *Extreme Ownership* – Jocko Willink and Leif Babin
- *Leaders Eat Last* – Simon Sinek

- *Turn the Ship Around!* – L. David Marquet
- *The 7 Habits of Highly Effective People* – Stephen R. Covey

Books on Risk, Uncertainty, and Systems

- *The Black Swan* – Nassim Nicholas Taleb
- *Antifragile* – Nassim Nicholas Taleb
- *Thinking, Fast and Slow* – Daniel Kahneman
- *Normal Accidents* – Charles Perrow
- *Managing the Unexpected* – Karl Weick and Kathleen Sutcliffe

Books on Strategy, Innovation, and Foresight

- *Competitive Strategy* – Michael Porter
- *Blue Ocean Strategy* – W. Chan Kim and Renée Mauborgne
- *The Innovator's Dilemma* – Clayton Christensen
- *Seeing Around Corners* – Rita McGrath

Crisis, Communication, and Ethics

- *Crisis Management* – Steven Fink
- *Thanks for the Feedback* – Douglas Stone and Sheila Heen
- *The Speed of Trust* – Stephen M. R. Covey

(You can adjust or localize this list over time as your own favorites evolve.)

Appendix B: Toolkits for Vigilant Leaders

This appendix gives you a quick index of the practical tools introduced throughout the book. You can turn each into a one-page checklist or worksheet for your team.

1. Threat Identification & Assessment Toolkit

From Chapters 2 and 6:

- **PEST Analysis Template**
  - Columns: Political, Economic, Social, Technological
  - Top 3–5 items highlighted across all four
- **SWOT Summary Page**
  - Strengths, Weaknesses, Opportunities, Threats
  - Three key actions: use strengths, reduce weaknesses, respond to threats
- **Scenario Planning Sheet**
  - 3–4 named scenarios, key assumptions, expected impacts, no-regrets moves, contingent options
- **Weak Signal Log**
  - Date, source, description, potential impact, next action

2. Industry Foresight Toolkit

From Chapter 3:

- **Industry Forces Map**
  - Top 3–5 forces shaping your field over the next 3–5 years
- **Competitor & Disruptor Map**
  - Incumbents, low-cost players, premium players, digital disruptors
- **Signal Panel List**
  - Key reports, journals, regulatory sources, and serious analysts you will track
- **Foresight Council Agenda**
  - Quarterly meeting outline: key trends, implications, decisions, and actions

3. AI Foresight Toolkit

From Chapter 4:

- **AI Use-Case Selector**
  - Problem, decision type, data available, expected value
- **Data Inventory Sheet**
  - What data you collect, where it lives, quality, access
- **Pilot Plan**
  - Objective, scope, metrics, timeframe, owner, go/no-go criteria
- **AI Guardrails Checklist**
  - Privacy, security, bias, explainability, human review points

4. Agile Execution Toolkit

From Chapter 5:

- **Agile Project One-Pager**
  - Vision, key outcomes, time frame, team members
- **Backlog Template**
  - Prioritized items, estimates, owner, status
- **Sprint Script**
  - Sprint length, planning agenda, daily stand-up questions, review and retrospective questions

5. Weak Signals & Early Warning Toolkit

From Chapter 6:

- **Signals & Surprises Agenda**
  - Monthly meeting questions: What has changed? What surprised us? What does it mean?
- **Early Warning Indicators Sheet**
  - For each major risk: indicator, threshold, data source, owner
- **Small Experiment Planner**

- Question, hypothesis, test, metrics, duration, decision point

6. Resilience Toolkit

From Chapter 7:

- **Top Risk Matrix**
  - Impact, likelihood, current controls, needed actions
- **Margin & Redundancy Checklist**
  - Financial, operational, and people margin status
- **Wargame Outline**
  - Scenario, team, roles, timeline, key decisions, lessons learned
- **Continuous Improvement Log**
  - After-action reviews, suggested improvements, implemented changes

7. Crisis Management Field Guide

From Chapter 8:

- **Crisis Triggers & Definitions**
  - Events that automatically activate crisis protocols
- **Crisis Team Roster**
  - Roles, primary and backup contacts, contact info
- **Initial Response Checklist**
  - Safety, containment, activation, initial communication
- **Message Framework**
  - What we know, what we're doing, how it affects you, what's next
- **Post-Crisis Review Template**
  - Timeline, what worked, what failed, root causes, structural changes

You can keep these as printable one-pagers, internal PDFs, or part of a leadership manual. The key is to use them, refine them, and make them your own.

About the Author

Ron is a transformational life and leadership coach, consultant, educator, and safety professional with a career that spans creative, operational, and high-responsibility environments.

He began his professional journey in the world of animation, working for Walt Disney Feature Animation with screen credits on films including *Mulan, Tarzan, Lilo & Stitch, The Emperor's New Groove, The Princess and the Frog,* and the "Human Again" sequence from *Beauty and the Beast.* That season taught him the power of disciplined creativity, teamwork, and long-term focus on excellence.

Ron later brought the same discipline to the world of health, fitness, and safety. He is:

- A Certified Personal Trainer with the American College of Sports Medicine
- A Corrective Exercise Specialist, Golf Fitness Specialist, and Fitness Nutrition Specialist with the National Academy of Sports Medicine
- A Certified American Heart Association CPR Instructor
- A Certified Fitness Safety Manager with the Fitness Law Academy
- A Certified Life Coach

He has worked extensively with individuals and organizations on physical performance, injury prevention, and risk management—always with a focus on **vigilance, responsibility, and long-term health**.

Beyond technical credentials, Ron is a transformational life coach and consultant who helps leaders align their values, habits, and strategies with the outcomes they actually want—in business, in health, and in family life. He is passionate about pro-American principles of personal responsibility, stewardship, and opportunity, and he brings that mindset to his work with executives, entrepreneurs, and teams.

Ron is the founder of **TrueShift.VIP**, a transformational consulting and coaching practice. Through TrueShift.VIP, he works privately with:

- Business owners and executives who want to lead with vigilance instead of constant reaction
- High achievers who want to build wealth without sacrificing their health, marriage, or integrity
- Organizations that want to create safer, stronger, more disciplined cultures

He also serves as an educator and mentor, including work as a substitute teacher in Orange County Public Schools in Florida, where he invests in the next generation with the same seriousness he brings to boardrooms and coaching sessions.

Ron is a husband and father, a student of American and military history, and a believer that leadership is a sacred trust. When he is not coaching or teaching, he is often reading history, refining his own training, or spending time with his family.

Work With Ron and TrueShift.VIP

Reading a book is a strong start. Real transformation happens when you apply these principles with accountability and tailored guidance.

Through **TrueShift.VIP**, Ron offers:

- **Private One-on-One Coaching**
  Focused guidance for leaders who want to sharpen their vigilance, build resilient wealth, and lead with strength at work and at home.
- **Executive and Leadership Team Coaching**
  Structured programs that help teams apply the frameworks in this book—PEST, SWOT, scenarios, Agile execution, resilience, and crisis management—to their specific organization.
- **Workshops and Keynotes**
  Live or virtual sessions on vigilant leadership, threat identification, industry foresight, safety and risk, and crisis-ready culture.

If you are serious about becoming a vigilant leader—and building an organization that can thrive in uncertainty—consider this your invitation to take the next step.

You do not have to do it alone.

Additional Resources

<u>Join Ron on Udemy for a suite of Vigilant Leadership courses:</u>

Visit Ron on Udemy by scanning this QR Code:

Visit Ron on LinkedIn Using this QR Code:

<u>Related Books:</u>

- **"Good to Great: Why Some Companies Make the Leap and Others Don't" by Jim Collins**
  Explores what makes some companies thrive while others fail, offering insights into building lasting greatness.
- **"Leadership in Turbulent Times" by Doris Kearns Goodwin**
  Provides historical examples of leadership during crises, offering timeless lessons for today's leaders.
- **"Dare to Lead: Brave Work. Tough Conversations. Whole Hearts." by Brené Brown**
  Focuses on the courage and vulnerability required to lead effectively, fostering a culture of trust and innovation.
- **"Start with Why: How Great Leaders Inspire Everyone to Take Action" by Simon Sinek**

Sinek's exploration of the power of purpose is key for leaders looking to inspire and motivate their teams.

- **"Primal Leadership: Realizing the Power of Emotional Intelligence" by Daniel Goleman, Richard Boyatzis, and Annie McKee**
Delves into the importance of emotional intelligence in leadership, aligning well with the discussions on EI in this book.

- **"Extreme Ownership: How U.S. Navy SEALs Lead and Win" by Jocko Willink and Leif Babin**
Offers practical leadership lessons from the battlefield, emphasizing accountability and decisiveness.

- **"Leadership on the Line: Staying Alive through the Dangers of Leading" by Ronald A. Heifetz and Marty Linsky**
Examines the challenges and risks of leadership, offering strategies for navigating difficult situations.

- **"The Leadership Challenge: How to Make Extraordinary Things Happen in Organizations" by James M. Kouzes and Barry Z. Posner**
A comprehensive guide to leadership practices that inspire and drive success.

- **"The Innovator's Solution: Creating and Sustaining Successful Growth" by Clayton M. Christensen and Michael E. Raynor**
Focuses on sustaining innovation and growth in organizations, complementing themes of strategic foresight.

- **"Drive: The Surprising Truth About What Motivates Us" by Daniel H. Pink**
Explores the science of motivation, offering insights for leaders on how to inspire and engage their teams.

Online Courses:

- **Transformational Leadership (LinkedIn Learning)**
  Learn how to inspire and guide transformational change in your organization.
- **Leading Through Crisis (Coursera)**
  Develop the skills to lead effectively through crises and uncertainty.
- **Advanced Emotional Intelligence (Udemy)**
  Enhance your emotional intelligence and apply it to leadership scenarios.
- **Decision Making and Problem Solving (edX)**
  Improve your decision-making processes with practical tools and frameworks.
- **Leading with Ethics and Integrity (FutureLearn)**
  Explore ethical leadership and how to navigate complex moral challenges.
- **Innovation Leadership (Coursera)**
  Foster a culture of innovation and drive growth within your organization.
- **Conflict Resolution and Negotiation (LinkedIn Learning)**
  Master conflict resolution techniques to foster a collaborative work environment.
- **Leading Change (edX)**
  Learn strategies for leading successful change initiatives within your organization.
- **Strategic Communication in Business (Coursera)**
  Improve your communication strategies to better engage and persuade stakeholders.
- **Crisis Communication Strategies (Udemy)**
  Develop effective communication strategies to manage crises and protect your organization's reputation.

Podcasts:

- **"The Art of Leadership" by Leadership Now Project**
  Insights and advice from top leaders on navigating the complexities of leadership.
- **"HBR Women at Work" by Harvard Business Review**
  Discussions on the unique challenges and opportunities faced by women in leadership.
- **"The Leadership Toolkit Podcast" by Leadership Development News**
  Practical tips and tools for enhancing your leadership capabilities.
- **"Leading Matters" by Jo Saxton and Steph O'Brien**
  Conversations on the intersection of leadership and life's challenges.
- **"The School of Greatness" by Lewis Howes**
  Interviews with successful individuals across various fields, sharing their lessons on leadership and success.
- **"Leadership Biz Café" by Tanveer Naseer**
  Exploring the human side of leadership with a focus on creating engaging workplaces.
- **"The EntreLeadership Podcast" by Dave Ramsey**
  Leadership advice for entrepreneurs and small business owners.
- **"The Leadership Advisor Podcast" by Rob Calise**
  Leadership lessons from experts across industries, focusing on practical application.
- **"Women Taking the Lead" by Jodi Flynn**
  Leadership advice and inspiration specifically for women in leadership roles.
- **"Leadership and Loyalty" by Dov Baron**
  Explores what it takes to build loyalty and trust as a leader.

Websites/Blogs:

- **McKinsey & Company Leadership Insights**
  (mckinsey.com/featured-insights/leadership)
  Research and insights on leadership trends and best practices.
- **Inc. Leadership Section**
  (inc.com/leadership)
  Articles and advice on leadership for entrepreneurs and business leaders.
- **Center for Creative Leadership Insights**
  (ccl.org/insights)
  Leadership research, articles, and tools for personal and organizational growth.
- **Mindful Leadership Blog**
  (mindfulleader.org/blog)
  Exploring the intersection of mindfulness and leadership.
- **Leaderonomics Leadership Articles**
  (leaderonomics.com/leadership)
  Practical advice and insights on leadership development.
- **Deloitte Leadership Insights**
  (deloitte.com/us/en/insights/leadership.html)
  Articles and studies on leadership challenges and strategies.
- **Leadership Freak Blog**
  (leadershipfreak.blog)
  Bite-sized leadership advice and reflections.
- **Fast Company Leadership Section**
  (fastcompany.com/leadership)
  News and insights on leadership, innovation, and creativity.
- **Tony Robbins Blog**
  (tonyrobbins.com/blog)
  Articles on leadership, personal development, and achieving success.
- **Leadership Now Blog**
  (leadershipnow.com)
  Resources and reflections on leadership excellence.

Professional Organizations:

- **International Society for Leadership Studies (ISLS)**
  A global organization dedicated to advancing leadership education and practice.
- **American Management Association (AMA)**
  Offers professional development and leadership training programs.
- **Executive Leadership Council (ELC)**
  A network for African-American executives dedicated to increasing diversity in leadership.
- **Leadership Development Association (LDA)**
  Focuses on the development of leaders at all organizational levels.
- **National Association of Corporate Directors (NACD)**
  Provides resources and education for board members and corporate directors.
- **International Leadership Association (ILA)**
  A global network focused on the study and practice of leadership.
- **Society for Industrial and Organizational Psychology (SIOP)**
  Focuses on the science and practice of workplace psychology, including leadership.
- **Center for Women in Leadership (CWL)**
  Aims to support and empower women in leadership roles.
- **Global Leadership Network (GLN)**
  Offers leadership training and resources with a focus on ethical leadership.

Journals/Research Papers:

- **Academy of Management Review**
  Scholarly research on management and organizational behavior.

- **Journal of Applied Psychology**
  Focuses on the application of psychological research in workplace settings.
- **Journal of Management**
  Covers research on all aspects of management and organizational theory.
- **Leadership & Organization Development Journal**
  Offers research on leadership development and organizational change.
- **Leadership Quarterly**
  Scholarly research on leadership theory and practice.
- **Journal of Leadership & Organizational Studies**
  Explores leadership in organizations and its impact on performance.
- **Organizational Dynamics**
  Research on organizational behavior, change, and development.
- **Journal of Business Ethics**
  Focuses on the ethical aspects of leadership and business practices.
- **Strategic Management Journal**
  Covers research on strategic management and organizational strategy.
- **Organizational Behavior and Human Decision Processes**
  Research on decision-making and organizational behavior.

Networking Events/Conferences:

- **World Business Forum**
  A global conference featuring world-class speakers on business and leadership.
- **Global Leadership Summit**
  An annual event focused on leadership development across sectors.

- **Women's Leadership Conference**
  Aimed at empowering women leaders with insights and networking opportunities.
- **Forbes Women's Summit**
  Brings together women leaders from various industries to share experiences and strategies.
- **The Leadership Circle Summit**
  Focuses on transformational leadership and development.
- **Lean In Leadership Summit**
  Based on Sheryl Sandberg's "Lean In," this event empowers women in leadership.
- **Global Leadership Conference (hosted by FranklinCovey)**
  A conference dedicated to developing leadership excellence worldwide.
- **CIO Leadership Summit**
  A leadership event for CIOs focused on technology and innovation.
- **Executive Leadership Summit**
  Brings together senior executives to discuss leadership challenges and solutions.
- **Leadership Excellence and Development Summit (LEADS)**
  Focuses on leadership development and excellence in organizations.

Are You Ready?

As you continue your journey towards becoming a vigilant leader, I encourage you to explore the wealth of resources listed in this appendix. These books, courses, podcasts, and events are designed to deepen your understanding of the concepts discussed in this book and to equip you with the tools necessary to navigate the complexities of leadership in today's rapidly changing world.

Moreover, I'm excited to announce that this book will be available as a comprehensive course on Udemy.com. This course will offer interactive lessons, practical exercises, and deeper dives into each chapter's concepts, providing you with a structured and engaging learning experience.

To stay on the cutting edge of your industry, commit to continuous learning and personal growth. Whether you're enhancing your emotional intelligence, mastering crisis management, or leading innovation, remember that the journey of leadership is one of constant evolution. By investing in your development and the growth of those around you, you'll not only become a more effective leader but also create lasting, positive change within your organization and beyond.

TOOLKITS FOR VIGILANT LEADERS

Risk Management Strategies:

Risk management involves identifying, assessing, and mitigating potential risks that could impact an organization's objectives, projects, or operations. Risk management strategies aim to minimize the likelihood and impact of negative events while maximizing opportunities for success. These strategies typically involve several key steps:

Risk Identification: Identifying potential risks and uncertainties that could affect the organization, including internal and external factors such as financial risks, operational risks, regulatory risks, and market risks.

Risk Assessment: Assessing the likelihood and potential impact of identified risks to prioritize them based on their severity and significance to the organization.

Risk Mitigation: Implementing measures to reduce or mitigate the impact of identified risks, such as implementing controls, diversifying investments, purchasing insurance, or developing contingency plans.

Monitoring and Review: Continuously monitoring and reviewing the effectiveness of risk management strategies to identify new risks, evaluate the success of mitigation efforts, and adapt strategies as needed to address changing circumstances.

Crisis Communication:

Crisis communication refers to the strategic communication efforts undertaken by an organization to manage and mitigate the impact of crises or emergencies on its reputation, stakeholders, and operations. Effective crisis communication involves:

Timely Response: Responding promptly to crises or emergencies as they arise, acknowledging the situation, and providing accurate information to stakeholders in a transparent and empathetic manner.

Clear Messaging: Communicating clear, consistent, and factual information to stakeholders to mitigate confusion, rumors, and misinformation. Messaging should be tailored to the needs and concerns of different stakeholders, including employees, customers, investors, and the public.

Stakeholder Engagement: Engaging with stakeholders proactively to address their concerns, provide updates on the situation, and solicit feedback and input to inform decision-making and response efforts.

Adaptability: Remaining flexible and adaptable in crisis communication strategies, adjusting messaging and tactics as the situation evolves and new information becomes available.

Scenario Planning: Scenario planning is a strategic planning tool that involves creating and analyzing multiple plausible future scenarios to anticipate and prepare for a range of possible outcomes. Scenario planning helps organizations:

Anticipate Change: Identify key uncertainties and trends that could impact the organization's future, such as technological advancements, market shifts, regulatory changes, or geopolitical events.

Develop Contingency Plans: Develop contingency plans and strategies to address different scenarios, including best-case, worst-case, and various alternative futures. This enables organizations to adapt quickly and effectively to changing circumstances and minimize the impact of unexpected events.

Test Assumptions: Challenge assumptions and biases about the future by exploring diverse scenarios and their implications. Scenario planning encourages organizations to think critically, creatively, and strategically about potential risks and opportunities, fostering a more proactive and adaptive approach to planning and decision-making.

Resilience Building: Resilience building involves strengthening an organization's ability to withstand and recover from adversity, disruption, and change. Resilience-building efforts focus on:

Adaptability: Cultivating a culture of adaptability and agility within the organization, enabling employees to respond effectively to unexpected challenges and seize opportunities for innovation and growth.

Resourcefulness: Developing robust systems, processes, and resources to support business continuity and minimize disruptions during crises or emergencies. This may include investing in redundancy, diversifying supply chains, and developing alternative work arrangements.

Employee Well-being: Prioritizing employee well-being and mental health to build individual and organizational resilience. Providing support, resources, and training to help employees cope with stress, uncertainty, and change can enhance overall resilience and productivity.

Learning and Improvement: Fostering a culture of continuous learning and improvement, where failures and setbacks are viewed as opportunities for reflection, adaptation, and growth. Encouraging open communication, feedback, and knowledge sharing helps organizations learn from past experiences and build resilience for the future.

Environmental Scanning:

Regularly scan the external environment for emerging trends, threats, and opportunities.

Utilize tools such as SWOT analysis, PEST analysis, and scenario planning to assess the business landscape.

Stay informed through industry publications, market research reports, and competitive intelligence.

Risk Assessment:

Conduct comprehensive risk assessments to identify potential threats and vulnerabilities.

Prioritize risks based on their likelihood and potential impact on the organization.

Develop mitigation strategies and contingency plans to address identified risks proactively.

Early Warning Systems:

Implement early warning systems to monitor key performance indicators and detect subtle changes in the business environment.

Utilize data analytics, dashboards, and automated alerts to identify anomalies and deviations from expected trends.

Establish triggers and thresholds for escalation in response to emerging risks or opportunities.

Scenario Planning:

Engage in scenario planning exercises to anticipate and prepare for potential future scenarios.

Explore a range of possible outcomes and develop contingency plans to address each scenario.

Involve key stakeholders in the scenario planning process to ensure diverse perspectives and insights.

Continuous Learning:

Foster a culture of continuous learning and self-improvement within the organization.

Invest in leadership development programs, training workshops, and educational resources to enhance strategic vigilance skills.

Encourage employees to pursue professional certifications, attend conferences, and participate in industry networking events.

Cross-Functional Collaboration:

Foster collaboration and information sharing across departments and teams.

Establish cross-functional task forces or committees to address strategic challenges and opportunities.

Leverage diverse perspectives and expertise to enhance strategic decision-making and problem-solving.

Stakeholder Engagement:

Maintain open lines of communication with key stakeholders, including employees, customers, suppliers, and investors.

Seek feedback and input from stakeholders to inform strategic decisions and priorities.

Build trust and credibility through transparent communication and accountability.

Adaptive Leadership:

Embrace adaptive leadership practices that prioritize flexibility, agility, and resilience.

Encourage experimentation, innovation, and creativity in response to changing circumstances.

Lead by example, demonstrating a willingness to learn, adapt, and navigate uncertainty with confidence.

Review and Reflection:

Regularly review and reflect on past experiences, decisions, and outcomes.

Conduct post-mortem analyses and lessons learned sessions to extract insights and identify opportunities for improvement.

Use feedback mechanisms to gather input from employees and stakeholders on leadership effectiveness and strategic direction.

Regular Evaluation and Adjustment:

Continuously evaluate the effectiveness of vigilance strategies and practices.

Adjust and refine the vigilance toolkit based on evolving business conditions, feedback, and lessons learned.

Stay agile and responsive to changing circumstances, iterating on strategies as needed to maintain a proactive and adaptive approach to leadership.

Checklist for Vigilant Leaders

Daily:

- **Scan the Environment:**
    - Monitor news, industry updates, and social media channels for emerging trends, threats, or opportunities.
    - Use AI tools and analytics platforms to aggregate and analyze relevant information, ensuring nothing critical is missed.
- **Review KPIs and Metrics:**
    - Assess key performance indicators (KPIs) and metrics to monitor the organization's health.
    - Pay special attention to any deviations from expected performance, and investigate root causes immediately.
- **Team Engagement:**
    - Check in with team members to assess progress on key initiatives and address any immediate concerns.
    - Foster open communication to ensure team members feel comfortable sharing challenges or innovative ideas.
- **Project Alignment:**
    - Evaluate the status of ongoing projects and initiatives to ensure alignment with strategic objectives.
    - Prioritize tasks that directly contribute to long-term goals and ensure resources are allocated effectively.
- **Reflection and Adaptation:**
    - Conduct a brief reflection session at the end of each day to identify unexpected developments or areas requiring further attention.
    - Be prepared to pivot strategies based on daily learnings, maintaining agility in decision-making.

Weekly:

- **Conduct Team Briefings:**
    - Hold weekly team briefings to review progress, address challenges, and celebrate wins.
    - Use these meetings to reinforce the alignment of day-to-day activities with the organization's strategic objectives.
- **Competitive Analysis:**
    - Perform a quick review of competitors' activities to stay ahead in the market.
    - Identify any shifts in the competitive landscape that could impact your organization's position.
- **Networking:**
    - Engage with industry peers and thought leaders through online forums, webinars, or networking events.
    - Build relationships that could offer insights or collaborations beneficial to your strategic objectives.

Monthly:

- **In-Depth Industry Analysis:**
    - Conduct a comprehensive analysis of industry trends, market dynamics, and the competitive landscape.
    - Use this analysis to identify potential opportunities or threats that may require a strategic response.
- **Risk Management:**
    - Review risk registers and assess the effectiveness of risk mitigation strategies.
    - Update the risk management plan based on new information or changes in the business environment.
- **Strategic Meetings:**
    - Schedule regular meetings with department heads to discuss performance, challenges, and opportunities.

- Ensure that all departments are aligned with the organization's strategic goals and that any cross-functional issues are addressed.
- **Progress Evaluation:**
  - Evaluate progress toward long-term goals and strategic priorities.
  - Adjust plans or strategies as necessary to ensure continued alignment with the organization's vision.
- **Professional Development:**
  - Engage in professional development activities to enhance leadership skills and strategic thinking capabilities.
  - Encourage team members to participate in learning opportunities that will benefit their roles and the organization.
- **Innovation Sessions:**
  - Hold monthly innovation sessions where team members can pitch new ideas or improvements.
  - Implement a process for evaluating and integrating viable ideas into strategic initiatives.

Quarterly:

- **Customer and Stakeholder Engagement:**
  - Conduct quarterly surveys or feedback sessions with customers and key stakeholders to gauge satisfaction and gather insights.
  - Use this feedback to refine products, services, and communication strategies.
- **Technology Review:**
  - Review the organization's technology stack and digital tools to ensure they are up-to-date and support strategic goals.
  - Consider adopting new technologies that could drive efficiency or create competitive advantages.

- **Scenario Planning:**
    - Engage in scenario planning exercises to anticipate potential disruptions and develop contingency plans.
    - Regularly stress-test business models against these scenarios to identify vulnerabilities and strengthen the organization's resilience.

Annual:

- **Strategic Review:**
    - Conduct a comprehensive strategic review to assess the organization's performance over the past year.
    - Evaluate the effectiveness of strategic initiatives and identify lessons learned for future planning.
- **Strategic Plan Update:**
    - Update the organization's strategic plan, incorporating new insights and adjustments based on changing conditions.
    - Align the strategic plan with emerging market trends and future projections.
- **Risk Management Overhaul:**
    - Conduct a thorough review of the organization's risk management practices.
    - Update risk mitigation strategies to reflect new risks identified over the year, ensuring they are comprehensive and proactive.
- **Goal Setting:**
    - Set goals and objectives for the upcoming year, ensuring they align with the organization's vision and strategic direction.
    - Include both short-term tactical goals and long-term strategic goals that drive the organization forward.
- **Leadership Development:**
    - Invest in leadership development programs for key leaders and managers.

- o Focus on areas such as strategic foresight, crisis management, and emotional intelligence to prepare leaders for future challenges.

A Call to Action:

By following this enhanced checklist, vigilant leaders can maintain a proactive stance, continuously adapting to new challenges and opportunities while steering their organizations toward sustained success. As you refine your leadership practices, consider incorporating these strategies into your daily, monthly, and annual routines. Remember, the key to vigilant leadership lies in the constant pursuit of knowledge, adaptability, and strategic foresight. Keep learning, stay agile, and lead with vision.

This checklist, along with the other strategies and insights discussed in this book, will be further explored in my upcoming Udemy course. Be sure to enroll to gain deeper insights and practical applications that will enhance your leadership journey.

Crisis Management Toolkit

Instructions for Leaders on Using the Crisis Preparedness and Management Plan:

Familiarize Yourself with the Plan:

Review the entire Crisis Preparedness and Management Plan thoroughly to understand its components, objectives, and procedures.

Ensure that you comprehend the roles and responsibilities outlined for the Crisis Management Team (CMT) and other stakeholders.

Conduct Risk Assessments:

Initiate regular risk assessment sessions to identify potential threats and vulnerabilities that could impact the organization.

Collaborate with relevant departments to evaluate the severity and likelihood of identified risks.

Establish the Crisis Management Team (CMT):

Select key individuals from various departments to form the Crisis Management Team (CMT).

Clearly define roles and responsibilities within the CMT to ensure efficient coordination and decision-making during crises.

Develop a Comprehensive Crisis Response Plan:

Work with the CMT to develop a detailed crisis response plan that outlines objectives, communication protocols, decision-making processes, and response strategies.

Ensure that the plan addresses various types of crises and includes provisions for both immediate response actions and long-term mitigation strategies.

Implement Communication Strategies:

Establish clear internal and external communication channels and protocols for disseminating information during a crisis.

Designate spokespersons and media relations contacts to manage external communication effectively.

Monitor and Evaluate:

Implement monitoring systems to track crisis events and evaluate the effectiveness of the response in real-time.

Conduct post-crisis evaluations to identify areas for improvement and update the crisis management plan accordingly.

Train and Prepare Your Team:

Provide regular training and development opportunities for the CMT and other employees on crisis response protocols.

Conduct scenario-based exercises and drills to ensure readiness and familiarity with crisis procedures.

Foster a Culture of Vigilance:

Lead by example by demonstrating a proactive approach to risk identification and crisis management.

Encourage employees at all levels to report potential risks and take swift, decisive actions when necessary.

Commit to Ongoing Improvement:

Regularly review and update the Crisis Preparedness and Management Plan to reflect changes in the organizational environment and lessons learned from past crises.

Encourage feedback from the CMT and employees to continuously improve the effectiveness of the plan.

By following these instructions and actively engaging with the Crisis Preparedness and Management Plan, you can enhance your organization's readiness to effectively navigate and mitigate crises, demonstrating vigilant leadership and ensuring the resilience and success of your organization.

Outline of a Crisis Preparedness and Management Plan

I. Introduction

A. Definition of a Crisis

B. Importance of Crisis Preparedness

C. Role of Vigilant Leadership in Crisis Management

II. Risk Assessment and Identification

A. Conducting Risk Assessments

    1. Identifying Potential Threats and Vulnerabilities
    2. Evaluating Impact and Likelihood of Risks

B. Developing Risk Profiles

    1. Prioritizing Risks Based on Severity and Probability
    2. Mapping Risks to Organizational Objectives

III. Crisis Management Team Formation

A. Establishing a Crisis Management Team (CMT)

    1. Selecting Key Stakeholders and Decision-Makers
    2. Designating Roles and Responsibilities within the CMT

B. Training and Preparation

    1. Conducting Regular Training Exercises and Simulations
    2. Ensuring CMT Members Understand Protocols and Procedures

IV. Crisis Response Plan Development

A. Creating a Comprehensive Crisis Response Plan

    1. Establishing Clear Objectives and Goals
    2. Developing Communication Protocols and Channels
    3. Identifying Key Stakeholders and Decision-Making Processes

B. Implementing Response Strategies

    1. Immediate Response Actions
    2. Short-term and Long-term Mitigation Strategies
    3. Resource Allocation and Coordination

V. Communication Strategies

A. Internal Communication Plan

1. Ensuring Clear Lines of Communication within the Organization
2. Providing Regular Updates and Information to Employees

B. External Communication Plan

1. Establishing Spokespersons and Media Relations Protocols
2. Communicating Transparently with Customers, Suppliers, and Stakeholders

VI. Crisis Monitoring and Evaluation

A. Establishing Monitoring Systems

1. Utilizing Technology for Real-time Monitoring of Crisis Events
2. Analyzing Key Performance Indicators (KPIs) for Crisis Response

B. Conducting Post-Crisis Evaluation

1. Identifying Lessons Learned and Areas for Improvement
2. Updating Crisis Management Plans Based on Evaluation Findings

VII. Team Preparedness and Training

A. Continuous Training and Development

1. Providing Regular Training on Crisis Response Protocols
2. Conducting Scenario-based Exercises and Drills

B. Fostering a Culture of Vigilance

1. Encouraging Proactive Risk Identification and Reporting

2. Empowering Employees to Take Swift and Decisive Actions

VIII. Conclusion

A. Summary of Key Points

B. Importance of Vigilant Leadership in Crisis Preparedness and Management

C. Commitment to Ongoing Improvement and Adaptation to Ensure Organizational Resilience

References

https://www.scruminc.com/2022-state-agile-report-takeaways/

https://www.cbsnews.com/sanfrancisco/news/coronavirus-pandemic-zoom-san-jose-eric-yuan/

ABOUT THE AUTHOR

Ron Betta is a visionary leader with a diverse and storied career that spans multiple industries and disciplines. With a foundation in production management and entertainment, Ron's journey has taken him from the creative hubs of Walt Disney Feature Animation to the pioneering world of Walt Disney Imagineering, and beyond, including EA Sports. His career is a testament to his passion for innovation, storytelling, and excellence.

As an Assistant Production Manager for Walt Disney Feature Animation, Ron played a pivotal role in the creation of several iconic animated classics, including *Mulan*, *Lilo & Stitch*, and *The Emperor's New Groove*. His contributions to these beloved films earned him screen credits and widespread recognition, solidifying his reputation as a dedicated and creative force in the animation industry.

Ron's talents also extended to the world of interactive entertainment as an Art Production Manager for EA Sports, where he contributed to the success of the *Madden NFL* and *NCAA Football* franchises. His work delighted millions of fans worldwide, showcasing his ability to bridge creativity with technology in dynamic ways.

At Walt Disney Imagineering, Ron's passion for storytelling and innovation came to life in the form of immersive experiences at Disney theme parks and resorts. His work on groundbreaking attractions captivated audiences and set new standards for entertainment, further demonstrating his commitment to pushing the boundaries of what's possible.

Beyond his achievements in entertainment, Ron has also made his mark as a best-selling Udemy instructor, sharing his extensive knowledge and expertise in fitness, personal development, and leadership with students across the globe. As a Certified Personal Trainer with the American College of Sports Medicine and a Fitness Safety Manager, Ron is dedicated to helping others achieve their health and wellness goals, while ensuring the safety and quality of fitness facilities.

Today, Ron resides in Orlando, Florida, with his wife and two sons, where he continues to pursue his passions for creativity, fitness, and lifelong learning. His diverse background, relentless pursuit of excellence, and commitment to inspiring others are the driving forces behind his ongoing work. Whether through his innovative projects, educational endeavors, or leadership insights, Ron Betta remains a beacon of inspiration, empowering others to reach their full potential and navigate the complexities of the modern world with confidence and foresight.

VIGILANT LEADERSHIP

www.ingramcontent.com/pod-product-compliance
Lightning Source LLC
Chambersburg PA
CBHW050214230526

45470CB00001B/388